Hmong Americans in Michigan

DISCOVERING THE PEOPLES OF MICHIGAN

Russell M. Magnaghi, *Series Editor*
Arthur W. Helweg and Linwood H. Cousins, *Founding Editors*

Ethnicity in Michigan: Issues and People
Jack Glazier and Arthur W. Helweg

African Americans in Michigan
Lewis Walker, Benjamin C. Wilson, Linwood H.
Cousins

Albanians in Michigan
Frances Trix

Amish in Michigan
Gertrude Enders Huntington

Arab Americans in Michigan
Rosina J. Hassoun

Asian Indians in Michigan
Arthur W. Helweg

Belgians in Michigan
Bernard A. Cook

Chaldeans in Michigan
Mary C. Sengstock

Copts in Michigan
Eliot Dickinson

Cornish in Michigan
Russell M. Magnaghi

Danes and Icelanders in Michigan
Howard L. Nicholson, Anders J. Gillis, and Russell M.
Magnaghi

Dutch in Michigan
Larry ten Harmsel

Finland-Swedes in Michigan
Mika Roinila

Finns in Michigan
Gary Kaunonen

French Canadians in Michigan
John P. DuLong

Germans in Michigan
Jeremy W. Kilar

Greeks in Michigan
Stavros K. Frangos

Haitians in Michigan
Michael Largey

Hmong Americans in Michigan
Martha Aladjem Bloomfield

Hungarians in Michigan
Éva V. Huseby-Darvas

Irish in Michigan
Seamus P. Metress and Eileen K. Metress

Italians in Michigan
Russell M. Magnaghi

Jews in Michigan
Judith Levin Cantor

Latinos in Michigan
David A. Badillo

Latvians in Michigan
Silvija D. Meja

Lithuanians in Michigan
Marius K. Grazulis

Maltese in Michigan
Joseph M. Lubig

Mexicans and Mexican Americans in Michigan
Rudolph Valier Alvarado and Sonya Yvette Alvarado

Norwegians in Michigan
Clifford Davidson

Poles in Michigan
Dennis Badaczewski

Scandinavians in Michigan
Jeffrey W. Hancks

Scots in Michigan
Alan T. Forrester

Serbians in Michigan
Paul Lubotina

South Slavs in Michigan
Daniel Cetinich

Swedes in Michigan
Rebecca J. Mead

Yankees in Michigan
Brian C. Wilson

Discovering the Peoples of Michigan is a series of publications examining the state's rich multicultural heritage. The series makes available an interesting, affordable, and varied collection of books that enables students and educated lay readers to explore Michigan's ethnic dynamics. A knowledge of the state's rapidly changing multicultural history has far-reaching implications for human relations, education, public policy, and planning. We believe that Discovering the Peoples of Michigan will enhance understanding of the unique contributions that diverse and often unrecognized communities have made to Michigan's history and culture.

Hmong Americans
in Michigan

Martha Aladjem Bloomfield

Michigan State University Press

East Lansing

♾ The paper used in this publication meets the minimum requirements of
ANSI/NISO Z39.48-1992 (R 1997) (Permanence of Paper).

Michigan State University Press
East Lansing, Michigan 48823-5245

Printed and bound in the United States of America.

20　19　18　17　16　15　14　　　1　2　3　4　5　6　7　8　9　10

LIBRARY OF CONGRESS CATALOGING-IN-PUBLICATION DATA
Bloomfield, Martha Aladjem.
Hmong Americans in Michigan / Martha Aladjem Bloomfield.
pages cm.—(Discovering the peoples of Michigan)
Includes bibliographical references and index.
ISBN 978-1-61186-119-8 (pbk. : alk. paper)—ISBN 978-1-60917-409-5 (ebook)
1. Hmong Americans—Michigan—Social conditions. 2. Hmong Americans—Michigan—Biography.
3. Hmong Americans—Cultural assimilation—Michigan. 4. Immigrants—Michigan—
Social conditions. I. Title.
F558.2.H55B76 2014
305.8959'720774—dc23
2013020461

Cover and interior design by Charlie Sharp, Sharp Des!gns, Lansing, MI
Cover image is of Tong Vue working in a garden as part of the Self-Help Garden Project of the Greater Lansing
Food Bank, a nonprofit organization. Photo is used courtesy of Martha Aladjem Bloomfield.

Michigan State University Press is a member of the Green Press Initiative and is
committed to developing and encouraging ecologically responsible publishing
practices. For more information about the Green Press Initiative and the use of
recycled paper in book publishing, please visit *www.greenpressinitiative.org*.

Visit Michigan State University Press at *www.msupress.org*

To all the courageous Hmong Americans who came as refugees to Michigan or who were born in Michigan who willingly shared their stories so that others can discover them and to all those Hmong Americans in Michigan whose stories have yet to be told. Thank you.

In Hmong culture, every person's story, rich or poor, young or old, influential or unknown, is told.

VINCENT K. HER

Contents

Acknowledgments

I would like to thank the many Michigan residents of Hmong descent who willingly and graciously told their invaluable first-person stories. They are the very first Hmong Americans in Michigan to share their courageous stories for others to read about their challenging journeys. They include: Maykao Lytongpao, teacher in Detroit schools and past president, Great Lakes Hmong Association; the late Tom Cheng Vue, founding board member, Hmong Family Association, Lansing; his wife Nanci (Yang) Vue, nurse and past president of the Hmong Family Association; Lian Xiong, Whitney Auto Air employee, Lansing; Kao Xiong, Whitney Auto Air employee, Lansing; Christine Xiong, daughter of Kao and Lian Xiong, granddaughter of Tong Vue, graduate of Michigan State University, past president of Hmong American Student Association (HASA), Michigan State University, and Material Handling Engineer, General Motors–Lansing Delta at Ryder; Tong Vue, mother of Lian Xiong; Dr. T. Christopher Thao, Pastor, Warren Hmong Alliance Church; Chue Kue, insurance salesman and president, Hmong Community of Metro Detroit; Tru Hang, retired central intelligence officer (CIA) and retired General Motors employee and his wife, Li Hang, Fenton; Fu Hang, son of Tru and Li Hang, and health industry businessman, Fenton; Ying and Chou Xiong, former owners of Thai Kitchen, East Lansing; Goe Sheng Xiong, Michigan State University graduate and past vice president

HASA, Michigan State University who now works for Blue Care Network of Michigan; and Kou Yang, former student at Michigan State University and past president of the HASA, and currently student at the University of Wisconsin, Milwaukee.

I would also like to thank the following people who helped in other invaluable ways by sharing very useful information through their firsthand experience working with Hmong Americans or conducting research about them. They include: Jonathan Webb, director, Frankenmuth Historical Association; Patricia Hepp, former director, Catholic Social Services, Lansing; Judi Harris, director, St. Vincent Catholic Charities Lansing; Nghia Tran, health coordinator, St. Vincent Catholic Charities; Chris Dancisak, cochair, sponsorship committee for St. Michael Church in Grand Ledge, and retired director of community relations, Michigan Historical Museum; Anne Raucher, former director of the Garden Project, the Greater Area Lansing Food Bank; Martha Ratliff, professor of linguistics, Wayne State University; Andrea Louie, associate professor, Department of Anthropology, Michigan State University; Anna Pegler-Gordon, professor, James Madison College, Michigan State University, and director of Asian Pacific American Studies Program; Marsha MacDowell, professor and curator of folk arts, Michigan State University Museum, and professor, Department of Art and Art History; Pearl Yee Wong, collections coordinator, folk arts, Michigan State University Museum; Lynne Swanson, collections manager for cultural collection and assistant curator of folk art, Michigan State University Museum; Mark E. Pfeifer, editor, Hmong studies internet resource editor and lecturer, anthropology, State University of New York, Institute of Technology, Utica, New York; Steve Gold, professor, Department of Sociology, Michigan State University; Joe Cousins, senior academic specialist emeritus, and advisor to HASA at Michigan State University; Sheng-mei Ma, professor, Department of English, Michigan State University; Burke Speaker, deputy director of communications, Migration Policy Institute, Washington, D.C.; Vincent Delgado, academic specialist for civic engagement, Michigan State University Residential College in the Arts and Humanities, and cofounder of the Refugee Development Center; Dawn Arwood, office manager, State of Michigan, Office of Refugee Services; and Russell M. Magnaghi, professor of history, Northern Michigan University, and series editor. Once again, I would like to thank the wonderful, supportive, patient editors and staff at Michigan State University Press for their continued support of my endeavors. They are always a pleasure to work with: Julie Loehr, assistant director and editor-in-chief, Kristine Blakeslee, Annette Tanner, Julie Reaume, Travis Kimbel, and Dawn Martin. Thank you also to Charlie Sharp, Sharp Des!gns, for his beautiful book design.

As always I would like to thank my many friends who support and believe in my endeavors and my family: my sons, Avi Climo and Simi Climo, my husband, Alan Bloomfield, and my dear mother-in-law Betty Bloomfield Soffin, who all cheer me on.

Timeline of the Hmong

5000 BCE	Hmong live in plains along Yellow River in China.
3000 BCE	Hmong migrate to southern China.
19th century	Hmong flee to Indochina.
1810	Hmong settle in Vietnam, Thailand, and southeast Burma.
1893	France establishes Indochina in Vietnam, Laos, and Cambodia.
1954	France withdraws from Indochina.
1955	United States creates Program Evaluation Office, a military organization incognito to advise the Royal Lao Army to fight against the Laotian Communist faction, the Pathet Lao.
1959	United States recruits Hmong to gather intelligence about North Vietnamese in Laos.
1960s–1975	United States mobilizes Hmong to fight the Secret War against the Pathet Lao Communists in Laos.

1969   General Vang Pao, whom the United States recruited, now
            has an army of 40,000 men.

1973   Royal Lao government and Pathet Lao implement cease-
            fire and end the Secret War.

1975   Americans airlift General Vang Pao and his military
            supporters and their families to Thailand to refugee camps.

            Tru Hang (former member of CIA) and family come to
            Richville, Michigan.

            Chue Kue, insurance salesman, comes to Detroit.

1976   Teng Vang and two of his younger cousins and Tong Her
            and family settle in Grand Ledge, Michigan.

1975–1998   About 130,000 Hmong resettle in the United States.

Late 1970s Refugee Re-settlement for St. Vincent Catholic Charities
            begins work with Hmong refugees in Greater Lansing area.

1981   Tru Hang, his brother-in-law, and nephew start the first
            Hmong-owned restaurant in the United States—Chee Peng
            in Petoskey, Michigan.

1983   The Self-Help Garden Project, part of the Greater
            Lansing Food Bank, begins to provide emergency food
            to individuals and families. Refugees including the
            Bhutanese, Burmese, Hmong, and many others rent plots
            to garden.

1983   C. Kurt Dewhurst, former director of the Museum at
            Michigan State University (MSU), and Marsha MacDowell,
            curator of folk arts at the same museum, document some
            of the earliest information about the Hmong refugees who
            came to Lansing area.

1984   Elizabeth K. Brabbs performs a Michigan State University
            research project evaluating Hmong/Lao American
            gardeners and finds that Hmong gardens tend to be better
            managed, more labor intensive, less capital intensive, and,

based on management ratings, more economically sound than their American counterparts.

1991   Tru and Li Hang's son Lt. Colonel Yee Chang Hang, born in 1969 in Laos, is the first Laotian Hmong to graduate from the United States Military Academy at West Point.

1996   Hmong American Student Association (HASA) begins at Michigan State University.

2004-2006   Last major waive of 15,000 Hmong refugees comes to United States.

2008   Clint Eastwood directs, produces, and stars in *Gran Torino*, first mainstream US film that features Hmong Americans. Filming occurred in Metro Detroit, including Highland Park, Center Line, Warren, Royal Oak and Grosse Pointe Park.

2008   T. Christopher Thao comes to Michigan to pastor at the Warren Hmong Alliance Church.

2010   5,924 Hmong Americans now live in Michigan.

The Frankenmuth Museum and the Frankenmuth Historical Association hold an exhibit on Hmong refugees.

2011   General Vang Pao dies on January 6, 2011, in Clovis, California.

2012   Hmong Americans now own and operate over one hundred restaurants in Michigan that have American, Chinese, and Thai foods on their menus.

2014   Lt. Colonel Yee Chang Hang becomes a Colonel in the US Army.

Preface

The Hmong Americans—elderly, middle-aged, and young—in Michigan who participated in the interviews in this book were particularly friendly and gracious. Some had come as refugees; others were born in the United States. Excerpts from these oral histories and follow-up email interviews appear throughout the book to complement the secondary research. These people talked about their experiences, struggles, challenges, hopes, and dreams for future generations. Historian Paul Hillmer said, "To understand any group of people, one must become acquainted with their stories."[1]

Primary and secondary research is essential to tell these people's history, particularly since they did not have their own written language to document their own history. The personal oral histories and the objective written histories provide a context for each other that are equally essential to tell the full Hmong story. More specifically, little written material was available for Hmong refugees in Michigan. Therefore, I talked with the Hmong refugees and their descendents in Michigan to learn their stories.

The Michigan residents of Hmong origin were grateful for the opportunity to share their stories, memories, and perspectives and were generous with their time. While extremely busy with their primary and extended families in Michigan and elsewhere in the United States, as well as work and school, they understood and appreciated the importance of this project as a way to

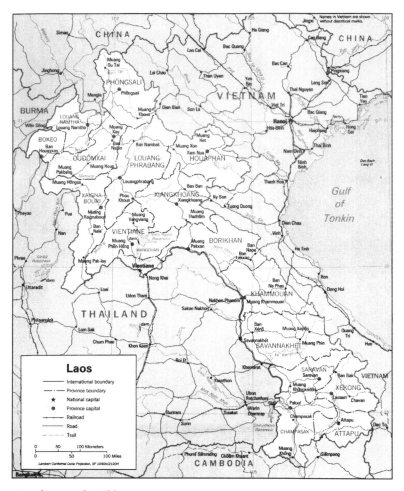

Map of Laos and neighboring countries.

tell the story of the Hmong people who found a new home in Michigan or who grew up here. They were patient and helpful with all my questions.

They talked about growing up in Laos, escaping through the jungle, crossing the Mekong River to Thailand, living in refugee camps in Thailand, coming to America, and adapting to their new home in Michigan. While they still have their painful memories of the past, they can now live in peace to pursue their goals and dreams without fear of persecution, war, drowning and other violent deaths, and loss of extended family.

Some were very young when they escaped from Laos to Thailand and then to the United States. The traumatic events in their lives were sometimes too painful or confusing to recall and share. Often, they did not fully understand what had happened during the chaos of the early years of their lives, but they still shared many of their life experiences. Their stories supported, complemented, and enhanced the existing histories of the Hmong people as told through other non-Hmong voices and other newly found Hmong voices.

At a Hmong New Year festival at the Ingham County Fairgrounds in November 2010, Maykao Lytongpao, then president of the Great Lakes Hmong Association, graciously offered her assistance for this project. She was the first Hmong American I met and interviewed. Fu Hang chaired the Michigan New Year and Cultural Festival in 2012; he was a consummate, warm host. While clearly overwhelmed by all the work required to organize and host the festival, and to house all extended family and friends from Michigan and Minnesota, Fu still found time to extend his hospitality. At his home in Fenton, Michigan, earlier that year I interviewed him and his father, Tru Hang, who had worked for the CIA back in Laos during the Secret War.

Over the course of two years, many of the interviewees for this book said that while growing up they could imagine that their lives might change one day. However, they could have never conceived just how much their lives would and did change—from living as subsistence farmers in the jungles of Laos, to the bare-bones refugee camps in Thailand, and then to the rural, urban, and suburban areas of Michigan in the twenty-first century.

I took photographs of the many cultural and athletic competition events at the New Year celebrations—all I had to do was smile and point to my camera, asking if it were all right to take photographs. The biggest smiles then came across each face—those of the young, middle-aged, and elderly, in contemporary Western clothes and traditional ethnic colorful outfits. Their eyes beamed. Each person's smile was warmer than the last one. In addition to interviewing Hmong Americans about their journeys, and members of churches and social organizations who worked with them when they came as refugees, I also conducted research based on a variety of written resources. They included books, articles, and reports written by museum curators, academics—historians, sociologists, anthropologists and professors of English, journalists who witnessed first-hand the life of the Hmong

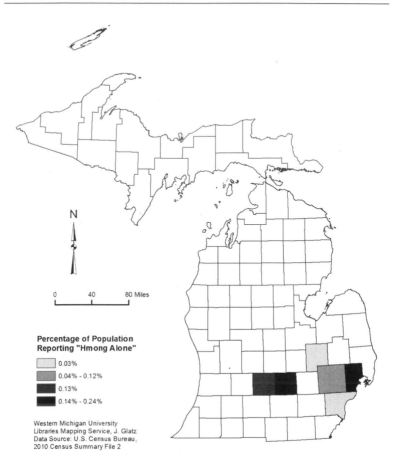

**Percentage of Population
Reporting "Hmong Alone"**

- 0.03%
- 0.04% - 0.12%
- 0.13%
- 0.14% - 0.24%

Western Michigan University
Libraries Mapping Service, J. Glatz
Data Source: U.S. Census Bureau,
2010 Census Summary File 2

people in Southeast Asia, and researchers for the United States government and private, non-profit agencies.

This particular book is merely an initial, very brief introduction to the Hmong Americans in Michigan, a backdrop or launch pad for others to explore Michigan residents of Hmong descent and to begin to discover these brave, innovative people. While a handful of stories of Hmong refugees and first-generation Hmong Americans in Michigan appear in this book, more than five thousand Hmong Americans live all over Michigan. They all have their stories to tell to complement and supplement their history in Laos and Thailand and their journey, adaptation, and contributions to Michigan.

Many people have written about the history of the Hmong in Southeast Asia and of Hmong Americans in the United States and, in particular, in Wisconsin, California, and Minnesota. However, other than the two books Marsha MacDowell, et al., that focus on the Hmong tapestries in Michigan, this book is the only one that specifically focuses on the history and culture of persons of Hmong origin in Michigan.

Read now to discover the Hmong American history and culture as revealed through a variety of perspectives. Explore their background history.

How did the Michigan residents of Hmong descent manage their lives, inspire their children, and thrive so very far away from home? How did they survive as others uprooted them so many times? How did they cope with the heavy emotional burden of the loss of so many relatives and friends from the war years and then carry so little with them on that long flight symbolically and literally to the United States? To travel some 8,560 miles from Bangkok, Thailand, to Michigan takes at least seventeen hours and forty-seven minutes by jet. Some still make the trip back to Laos and Thailand to visit relatives and friends who survived and remained. Some now even go to China to visit extended family.

Given their repeated trauma, memories and flashbacks, how do they fall asleep each night without fearing what might happen when they awaken? How do they get up each morning and face the new day knowing where they have been, adapt to their new environment, and try to discover new paths to explore and follow in their strange, new world?

A Brief Overview of Hmong History

The Hmong are a people who have no country of their own. For centuries, they have migrated thousands of miles and struggled as a minority to survive wherever they have lived. Not having a written language, they have relied on oral communications to maintain strong connections with family and friends in different countries across continents. While the Hmong traditionally lived far away from modern society with its conveniences of transportation and resources, they created a very strong "sense of kinship and community."[a]

Each ethnic group of people in the world is unique. However, the Hmong are particularly special because of their extraordinary history of migration, loyalty to one another, prolonged abuse, trauma, suffering from those who dominated them, profound loss, independence, and amazing capacity to adapt and remain resilient over centuries.

Who are these little-known people who number about seven million in the world? Where did they originate? Where and why have they traveled? Why do they have a special and unusual relationship with America? Where do they live now? What is their culture like? What work do they do? How and why did they come to America and specifically Michigan? What challenges have they had adapting to different cultures and environments? What are their lives like in the diaspora?

Originating presumably in China, many Hmong escaped to the south of China because of extreme persecution, then to Laos and Thailand. Throughout their history, the Hmong fled for their survival from those who wanted to dominate or kill them individually and collectively and to destroy their culture and way of life. They have suffered from disease, starvation, torture, and separation from family and friends. Over hundreds and even thousands of years, they have constantly experienced major dramatic change in their lives—geographic, economic, religious, social, and political. They have sought safe havens in each of the new countries to which they fled to protect themselves so they could work and raise their families.

When I asked one young woman, "Please forgive my ignorance, but how do you know when you first meet someone that that individual is of Hmong descent and not a member of another Asian ethnic group, before you ask them?" She said, "I can just feel it. I get goose bumps. I just know they are Hmong. And then we talk more and we put the pieces together."

As a minority culture, Hmong Americans in the past adapted to the larger, more dominant hostile communities with different customs, traditions, languages, religions, and political views. Despite the tremendous losses they have suffered for many years, they have remained strong and courageous with indomitable spirits, courage, and profound resilience. While the Hmong struggled for years to survive unimaginable challenges within China, European colonialism in Southeast Asia, and America's "empire building," they then came as refugees to the United States in the mid-1970s and have worked consistently "to maintain their ethnic identity."[3]

Between 1975 and 2006, several waves of Hmong refugees came to the United States. At first, about 130,000 Hmong refugees came here. Increased Hmong birthrates account for a much higher American Hmong population.[4] Beginning in the summer of 2004, the most recent group of 15,000 Hmong refugees came to resettle in the United States.[5] The Hmong Americans' status in the United States is as a "double minority—a minority within the Asian American community and in American society."[6]

Today, the Hmong live on five continents throughout the world including Asia, Europe, North America, South America, and Australia. The majority of them—four to six million—still live in mainland China. According to the 2010 US Census, about 260,076 Hmong live throughout the United States. Most of them live in California (91,224), then Minnesota (66,181), Wisconsin

(49,240) and North Carolina (10,864). Michigan has the fifth largest population of Hmong (5,924).[7]

Before discussing how and why the Hmong came to America and specifically how they came and adapted to Michigan, I will first paint an overview of their past, complex journey, and origins, and highlight a few of the myriad of key historical events. In that way, readers can better understand Hmong American lives as individuals and a people and as part of a much larger picture of world history that relates to Southeast Asia and the United States.

Hmong Americans are relatively new in the United States, as they only began to immigrate in mid-1975. Their stories are still fresh in their memories as they continue to forge their way in this country and provide opportunities to their children. Some were born in Laos, others in Thailand. Those young adults born in the United States talk about their challenges as children of immigrants as they developed friendships with others and pursued their education and jobs.

Scholars have shared interesting stories about whether or not the Hmong ever had a written language. Some say the Hmong once had one but that the Chinese threatened them with death if they used it. Since the Hmong were always running for their lives, they lost their ability to write down their language.[8] People who had a written language had an easier time dominating those who did not.[9] Folktales portray Hmong women weaving their letters into patterns on their dresses.[10] In the 1950s, missionaries began to write down the Hmong oral language in the Western alphabet.[11]

Paul Hillmer describes the complicated significance of the 'absence of a written language' and the importance of conducting careful oral history interviews when recounting Hmong history.

> Though we tend to think of oral history as history shared by word of mouth, it is more correctly defined as the history of people's memories. And as study after study has shown, the human memory is a notoriously unreliable or at least incomplete source. . . .
>
> Nonetheless, Hmong oral history is valuable and perhaps on average a little more reliable than accounts provided by Westernized, modernized minds. First, in the absence of a written language, their reliance on memory and oral communication makes it more rather than less likely that they

would remember specific details. Second, the intensity of their lives and frequent traumas they endured increase the likelihood that Hmong who lived in Laos can't forget what they experienced—even if they want to.[12]

However, since the Hmong came to the United States, many have become scholars, educators, artists, and community activists, and they are now, for the first time, writing about their own history, including autobiographies, memoirs, and poetry. They have written histories about their people in books and journal articles. This has been a profound phenomenon.[13]

Kao Kalia Yang was born in Ban Vinai refugee camp and came, as a refugee, with her parents to the United States. Currently, she teaches writing at the University of Wisconsin–Eau Clair. She returned temporarily to Thailand to explore her past. "My return to America was the landing of a new life direction, and an affirmation of a burning motivation, awareness of a life-giving wellspring of courage to do something I had not known that we Hmong people needed to do: speak and write our individual stories in search of a greater, fuller understanding of our shared experience. I had learned that each human being finds his or her home through telling life stories; that anyone who tried to take away a story trespasses in our heart's territory; that everyone who invites the telling of a tale hereby offers a welcome to home."[14]

How and why did they leave several homelands filled with brutality and warfare before coming to the United States? What challenges did they face as they resettled in Michigan? How did they adapt to strange new lives, thousands and thousands of miles away from where they grew up—and preserve their past through time and place, move their lives forward, and cultivate their dreams and hopes for their children and their education?

The Hmong Migrate to China: 3000 BCE

While the Hmong may have originated in Mesopotamia or Siberia, the best documented history states that they probably originally lived "in the plains along the Yellow River in China more than five thousand years ago." To protect themselves from Chinese persecution, the Hmong migrated to the mountains in southern China around 3000 BCE. Throughout their history, they usually moved because people dominated them and punished them with unfair taxes, slavery, and "ethnic persecution."[15]

> Hmong folktales describe a place having six months of light and six of dark, where snow lay on mountains and ice covered lakes. Over many centuries, they migrated eastward descending through northeast Tibet and then into southern China. There, the Chinese referred to them as *Miao* (*Meo* in Southeast Asia), sometimes translated as "barbarians," but actually a variation on the word "man." Their name for themselves—Hmong—means "people" although recently for political reasons, it has been translated as "free people."[16]

The earliest written accounts about the Hmong are in Chinese records from the third century BCE that report that the Hmong people rose up against the Chinese, who thought they were barbarians who needed civilizing. The Chinese drove them off their rice fields near the Yangtze and Yellow Rivers. In the sixth century, Hmong leaders formed a kingdom in the central Chinese provinces of Hunan, Hubei, and Henan that lasted a few hundred years until the Chinese destroyed it. The surviving Hmong then fled to Guizhou, Yunnan, and the mountains of Sichuan, where almost four to six million of them still live today.[17]

Many Hmong in the diaspora have yearned to visit their ancestors' homelands. More recently, since relations between China and the Hmong in the diaspora have improved, they have been able to visit. Some have traveled to places in China where no Hmong outside China have ever been.[18] Some Hmong who live in the United States have made contact with those Hmong living in other countries in the diaspora including Australia, Argentina, Canada, Germany, and France.[19]

The Hmong Bond with the French, Nineteenth Century

By the early nineteenth century, thousands of Hmong had left China and migrated to Burma, Laos, Vietnam, and Thailand. They practiced slash-and-burn farming. The Hmong hunted animals, raised livestock, and grew vegetables and fruits. Their main crop was opium poppies. While they maintained their separateness from the majority populations, they kept their connections to Hmong in other countries "through a shared religion, language, and history of persecution," similar to the Jews in Eastern Europe.[20] The Lao, Vietnamese, and Thai incorporated the Hmong into their societies by taxation.[21] Other than that, the Hmong remained separate.

By the late nineteenth century, French colonialists who were interested in the opium trade developed a special form of alliance with the Hmong in Laos. They wanted to compete with the British, who already had a relationship with China.[22] After the French realized that the Communists had taken over northern Laos, they signed an agreement with Ho Chi Minh in North Vietnam and left the area in July 1954.[23] The French relationship with the Hmong was a precursor for the United States befriending and recruiting the Hmong to fight the "Secret War" against the Communists in Laos.

The Hmong Ally with Americans, 1959

The United States believed that communism had to be contained.[24] In 1959, the United States recruited Hmong agents to gather intelligence about the North Vietnamese in Laos. In 1961, James William (Bill) Lair worked for the US Central Intelligence Agency (CIA). He recruited and trained ethnic minorities to fight the Vietnamese and Lao Communists.[25] President Kennedy sent special troops to Laos to train Royal Lao Army soldiers.[26] This practice went on for years. This involvement, kept secret from the American public, became "America's clandestine war in Laos."[27]

Understanding the importance of collaborating with powerful foreigners, Lieutenant Colonel Vang Pao, a Hmong soldier, and member of the Royal Lao Army rose to power. He wanted to protect the Hmong people from the Pathet Lao Communist forces. In exchange for supporting the American plan, he received military and humanitarian aid for the Hmong. Vang Pao became a general. In 1961, his army began with nine thousand men, and it grew to forty thousand by 1969.[28]

The US embassy in Laos collaborated with the CIA in the Secret War. The military base was at Long Cheng. To cover up the military operation, the United States Agency for International Development (USAID) had a hospital and school about twelve miles from Long Cheng. When US policymakers visited the area, the USAID officials showed them the humanitarian operation

Tru Hang as a soldier in Laos. Photo courtesy of Tru Hang.

Tru Hang (far right) with his friends Chai Ya Lee (far left) and Neng Sho Xiong (middle) at the Michigan New Year and Cultural Festival 2012 in Pontiac. These three men fought together in the Secret War in Laos. Photo by the author.

to prevent them from seeing the military involvement in Laos.[29] The Hmong might have hoped that fighting communism would raise their status in Laos, but unfortunately, they lost thousands of men and young boys.[30]

In 1970, eight years after the Secret War began, a *Time/Life* correspondent, Timothy Allman, and a French reporter exposed the operation, which set in motion outsiders' fascination with Long Cheng and the Hmong

Tru Hang and His Son, Fu Hang, Come to Michigan

Tru Hang and his family were some of the earliest Hmong refugees who came to Michigan due to his connection with the US military in Laos. He was a military intelligence officer in communications for the CIA at Long Cheng airbase. Currently, he lives with his wife, Li, and one of their sons, Fu Hang, and his family in Fenton, Michigan. He worked for General Motors for almost thirty years; beginning as a janitor, then on the assembly line, and finally as a machine operator. He has also opened many restaurants in Michigan.

Tru and Li Hang have eight children, all of whom have received a college degree. The third oldest, Yee Chang Hang, is the first Laotian Hmong to graduate from the US Military Academy at West Point and is still serving on active duty with the US Army. On March 3, 2014, Yee Chang Hang was raised to the rank of Colonel.

Fu Hang was five years old when he came with his family to Michigan. He now works in the health care industry. He said, "It was a very unsettling environment in Laos. Communism was the name of the game."

When Tru Hang was a teenager in the 1950s in Laos, his family lived on the road between Vietnam and Laos and practiced slash-and burn-farming—always on the move. They lived in the jungle, without running water or cars. In 1955, it took him half a day to walk to a school run by Laotians. "I saw war all my life. I met American people. Around 1958–60, I knew about Americans coming to

guerrilla fighters. Furthermore, refugee stories of heavy US bombing made it difficult for American officials to continue to deny their military activities in Laos. Once upon a time, the Hmong had been self-sufficient, but then they became dependent on the US government for food, education, employment, and business opportunities that profoundly altered their lives. After the Paris Agreement on Vietnam of January 27, 1973, the Royal Lao government and the Pathet Lao ended the war on February 21, 1973.[31]

Refugee Camps Open in Thailand, 1975

After the Pathet Lao and the Royal Lao governments agreed to a cease-fire to end the war in 1973, the Hmong and other minorities who had collaborated teach people to grow trees, apples, oranges and to raise pigs and chickens. By 1961, I saw Americans shipping guns, dropping supplies. The Americans sent me to school to learn English. I could then speak with the CIA people. I went to train in Thailand to become a radio operator, doing information reporting for the CIA."

Fu Hang said that because his father had been in the CIA, they all flew by helicopter from Vientiane, the capitol of Laos, to Thailand.

"Some people gave opium to their kids. I've heard stories that some kids were deserted. There are stories where young couples couldn't go on anymore. They left their child there so that they have the energy to go themselves. We heard stories of fathers leaving their children hidden in the banana leaves. The child then found his father in this country and to this day, the father has never said, 'I'm sorry.' We, my family, had it so good."

According to the Frankenmuth Historical Association in Michigan, while the Hang family was in the refugee camp, missionaries visited them and converted them to Christianity. Tru's brother-in-law had previously come to the United States through sponsorship of the St. Lorenz Congregation in Frankenmuth and other local sponsors. Tru's family members and concerned local citizens made connection with St. Michael's Church in Richville who sponsored him and his family over time. Tru continued the missionary spirit by helping financially to sponsor the immigration of five other Hmong families to the United States.

with the United States needed to find a safe haven. It took two years for a peaceful resolution to the conflict even after the formal end of the fighting.[32]

In May 1975, the Americans airlifted General Vang Pao, his military supporters, and their families to a military base in Thailand and eventually to the United States. The Americans sent cargo planes to assist Vang Pao's supporters to escape. Thousands of other Hmong people were upset because their military leaders were leaving them; they were frightened and did not know what the future would bring. They had taken whatever they could with them. Others fought for spaces on the planes. Sometimes they threw their children onto the planes and then tried to climb into the planes themselves.[33]

Initially, only about 2,500 Hmong could get on the flights from Laos to Thailand. Those who could not, fled Laos by foot and taxi. They did not want

Chue Kue Leaves Camp

Chue Kue, a translator and an insurance salesman in Warren, Michigan, came as a refugee to Detroit in 1975, having grown up in Long Cheng, Laos. He is president of the Hmong Community of Metro-Detroit, Inc., a nonprofit organization whose mission "is to empower the Hmong children and families of Michigan to achieve lifelong successes and improve the Hmong Community with the help of effective action and leadership of trained professionals and volunteers."

Kue reflected on his early years growing up in Laos during the war. "As a young boy, I expected my life to change in many ways, but I never imagined that I would have to move across the globe. My father worked for a special unit. He flew a plane from village to village, purchased rice, and distributed it to the refugees who moved from place to place because of the war. My mother stayed home and raised the family."

Kue had to get up very early in the morning to walk to school. When the cold days came, he would get up extra early to heat rocks that he wrapped with papers and put in his pockets to keep his hands warm. The after-school program was running back home, and that was plenty of good exercise.

"The challenge was when we traveled with the older kids. I was younger than the rest of the group. When they started running, I had to catch up with them or be left behind. I could not travel alone because the days were getting darker and there were lots of graveyards on the way. My darkest moment was when my three cousins died at war. I was very young and could not comprehend what was going at that time. All I saw were people crying everywhere. That was the most difficult time in my life."

Chue Kue said he was about fourteen or fifteen years old when he left Laos to go to Thailand. He traveled by foot with his brother, a few cousins, and friends. They traveled at night, passing through villages and the jungle.

Swimming across the Mekong River was quite an experience for me. I was frightened, confused, and nervous. So many thoughts and feelings went through my mind. What if we get killed? Should we go? Why did I leave my family behind? What is the good out there for me anyway?

In reality, it is safer to follow animal tracks or trails instead of following the regular trail. I did not see any elephants. If you see an elephant, it will be too close and you will get attacked by elephants. Sometimes, I was scared and sometimes not. I wanted to see the elephants with my own eyes. I imagined how elephants chased us, and how we would handle a situation. We traveled in a very big jungle on very high mountains after mountains.

Actually, it was very beautiful out there. We could only hear all kind of birds singing, animals crying, and the sound of nature itself. It was very peaceful and quiet."

Kue says they had to travel away from the villages so the Communist soldiers would not see them. He went to Ban Vinai refugee camp for a month and then moved to Nong Khai. He then learned that his family had reached Vinai, and he reunited with them there. The camp did not have a school, so he paid a private tutor to teach him English. He and his friends played volleyball and soccer for money. Once in awhile, they "snuck out of camp." If they did not get caught, they were very happy, but if they did, the Thai officers beat them up.

"The difficult time in camp was that we couldn't go outside of the camp. We got locked in at the camp just like a whole bunch of animals in the zoo. There was nothing to do except eat and play. The younger generation was looking forward to leaving the country to find their new homes, but the older generation was homesick and wanted to go back to their homeland. At first, I was confused, and I began to ask myself a question: 'What am I doing here?'"

Chue Kue told his family that he "would have to move on because there was no life in camp."

"It was very difficult and lonely to be separated from my family. There was nothing much that I could do. I could only pray that they will be safe."

Chue Kue wishes that the US government had had a program to teach all the refugees in the camp the American way of life and the basic language before coming to the United States so they would not have had such a hard adjustment to life here.

to call attention to their escape, so some left elderly and children family members behind. Thousands of them traveled through mined jungles. Some paid high fees to boat owners to transport them across the Mekong River on the border of northern Laos and Thailand. While some succeeded in entering Thailand, others died on route. Many Hmong initially believed they would and could remain in Laos, but then realized that the Communists would punish and kill them for collaborating with the Americans. They walked miles through the mountains and rain forests until they finally crossed the Mekong Delta.[34]

> "An estimated 35 percent died during their flight from illness, drowning, starvation, jungle accidents, or Pathet Lao forces. . . . The Hmong seldom had time to bury their dead, who were left to rot where they fell; often the ill and wounded were also left behind." . . . the lack of proper funeral and burial processes lead to the refugee's [*sic*] stress and guilt. They are afflicted with "bereavement overload": "The intensity of such bereavement might be expected to increase exponentially when the losses that follow each other in rapid succession include not only deaths, but also losses in status, possessions, familiar surroundings, and separation from loved ones."[35]

In Kao Kalia Yang's memoir she writes,

> When the Americans left Laos in 1975, they took the most influential, the biggest believers and fighters for democracy with them, and they left my family and thousands of others behind to wait for a fight that would end for so many in deaths. A third of the Hmong died in the war with the Americans. Another third were slaughtered in its aftermath. . . .
>
> The communist Pathet Lao soldiers and their north Vietnamese allies infiltrated Hmong villages and began a systematic campaign to kill off the Hmong who believed in the tenets of democracy and had fought against communist rule. While many of the 30,000 Hmong men and boys recruited by the CIA of the United States had been killed, the remnants of their fight remained in the hearts and the homes of their wives and children, their mothers and fathers, their friends and neighbors. The Secret War, the biggest covert operation in CIA history, and its ramifications would tear into the history of a people, break into the pages of their lives, and let the winds

Lian Xiong's husband, Kao, was born in Long Cheng. At seventeen or eighteen years old he joined the army. Kao did not have much time to go to school. As the oldest son, he helped grow food—sticky rice, corn, and vegetables—and raised chickens, cows, and pigs. Sadly, Kao's parents and sister never made it to Thailand: "I never saw my parents again. They drowned in the Mekong River—my mother, father, sister. Before they tried to cross the Mekong, my friend went back to Laos in 1976, secretly, and took a photo of my family." Kao has only this one photograph of his family in Laos. Photo courtesy of Kao Xiong.

of war and earth blow them all over the world. . . .

The Hmong knew that the Americans had left: one day there were American pilots landing planes on the airstrip, tall men with fair skin walking around the village, laughing and buying local food items, giving candy to the small children. And then one day the planes flew away into the fog of the clouds, passed over the dark green mountaintops, and did not return. At first, they waited. When the murders started, and the last of the men and boys began disappearing, the Hmong knew that the only thing coming for them was death.[36]

The Hmong refugees who fled to Thailand had a profoundly traumatic, devastating journey. They took whatever belongings they could. Less than

Lian and Kao Xiong Flee to Michigan

Lian Xiong was born in a village in northern Laos in 1958; her father was the province leader. She lived in Laos until she was about fifteen years old, then escaped to Thailand, where she lived in refugee camps. She and her husband, Kao, both work at Whitney Auto Air in Lansing, Michigan, where they repair parts for commercial airplanes. Lian graduated from Waverly High School and raised seven children, all of whom have completed college except for their youngest one, who is still in college. Some have also earned their master's degree. They live with many of their family members in St. Johns. ˙

Lian said that as she was growing up, she heard that the Communists were coming. She had many hardships during the war. Her family had to move from place to place. Sometimes they came back to the village when they thought it would be safe. Sometimes she went to school and sometimes she did not. "We hid out a little bit in the jungle. My parents gave us a little container of rice. We kept the rice close to us. If the enemy came close, we grabbed what we had so we didn't go hungry if we got lost in the woods. They would take everything."

Her family got used to moving around and was always on the alert. It did not matter whether it was night or day. When they heard the signal, "a certain sound from people's mouths" on this mountain or that path, they knew it was time. They knew the enemy was coming and they had to hide. Her parents would say, "It's time." The chickens also had to hide.

I did not actually see the enemy. My dad was a soldier before he became a clan leader. Kids went as soldiers to war. Probably not a single week passed that a dead body did not return to the village. We always had a fear of death. I saw ugly bodies wrapped in things. When they brought the bodies, as children, we raced to see who it was. Somebody else—it's your brother, your cousin. Lots of bodies. If the enemy comes, they would kill everybody. We always had a fear in our mind. Then you have to go to the army whether you like it or not. From 1961 to 1975, we lost 35,000 Hmong soldiers. Everything depended on the CIA. The war ended. The country has changed. The Vietnamese took over the country. The Lao government could not take care of the Hmong people. We had to leave. Mostly the leaders had to go. But we didn't have a way to go.

Lian and her family were in the first group to leave Laos for Thailand. While she was afraid, she said it was not as bad as the trying times in Laos. They grabbed whatever they could take and left everything else, got on buses, and paid people to help them. "My father left first. He fled like a bird. He left us behind. He was so scared. A second person helped him get on the bus. He impersonated a poor person in old, old clothes. Otherwise, they would kill him because he had fought in the army. We told him, 'Dad, if we are lucky, we'll see each other again. Otherwise, it's the end.' We found a way to cross and we found Dad."

Lian and her family walked from their village to take two buses to Vientiane, the capitol of Laos. The Hmong people were trying to cross the Mekong River secretly. Her mom found somebody to help them, but Lian, her siblings, and mother were all afraid that they would not get to the other side of the river to Thailand. She said they could not trust anyone. "We had three possibilities. The Lao boat people could take your money and not take you across the river; or they could take your money and dump you in the middle of the river and take more people; or they could be honest and take you across to Thailand."

Her family hid in the bushes. The boatman told them that if they see his boat and see him fishing, that was the signal and they should run as fast as they can. They had to look for the right time because the enemy was around the river. "We were the lucky ones. I pretended I was a fisherman. Sometimes, the Lao people came back and helped you. Sometimes the Thai people saved you."

Lian Xiong recalled her life in the Ban Vinai refugee camp from late 1975 to 1980. She and Kao were married and her first two children born there. "At first, the camps were open and we farmed. Then they closed off the camp so no one could work. They fed us. We had much hardship and no way to work. I did embroidery, *pa ndau*, for clothes particularly on rainy days when we couldn't do anything else."

When Lian was getting ready to leave for the United States, she said, "I feel like I'm dreaming." But she was also fearful. She was accustomed to working and living off the land, and she could not conceptualize life in an apartment with one plant. "How will I ever live with one pot of flowers?" she wondered.

half the refugees reached Thailand. Some were arrested. Others became sick or died from hunger and fatigue.[37] "Thai officers forced Hmong families back into Laos, beat them up, or even killed them on the spot if they did not have money to pay for their passage. Thai patrols raped many Hmong women and girls. Others were ransomed for money to pay for their family's passage. Laotians also took advantage of the Hmong."[38]

Many of the refugees also reported to the physicians and refugee camp workers that the Communists had attacked them from airplanes with a toxic chemical that later became known as "Yellow Rain." They said that because of exposure to the chemical, thousands of family members and friends had died or experienced severe health problems. The validity of these claims became a major political issue that officials have discussed and debated at the United Nations, the US Congress, the CIA, and in the media. Unfortunately, the issue has still never been resolved.[39]

From May to December 1975, over 44,000 Hmong refugees fled to Thailand. The numbers declined for a while and began to rise again in 1978. They received food and other humanitarian aid. While in the camps, they had nothing to do.[40] Over time, life got a little better when the United States provided more aid to Thailand. The Hmong also created schools, markets, and businesses.[41]

To discourage Hmong immigration into Thailand, Thai authorities made life extremely difficult for the Hmong. They encouraged "emigration out of it, to resettlement or, if possible, to repatriation."[42]

Because the Hmong had had to bribe the river boatmen and Thai patrols to cross the border, they had few belongings and little cash for food, shelter, or other basic human necessities once they arrived at the refugee camps in Thailand in the 1970s:[43] "Their world has been shattered. They are in passage, no longer Laotian, certainly not Thai, and not quite sure where they will end up or what their lives will become."[44]

"They became a people without a home, land or freedom."[45] Unfortunately, life was extremely difficult if not unbearable for the Hmong in the refugee camps in Thailand. While it was a dramatic change from Laos, the Hmong still did not have their own home. Now, another ethnic group tortured them and treated them inhumanely. They had little or nothing to do in the camps. Thai guards treated the Hmong like inmates in a prison.

"The Hmong refugees could not farm, work or travel freely in Thailand.

. . . Thai officers often beat, jailed, and fined anyone who left the camp without permission." The United Nations High Commissioner for Refugees (UNHCR) became responsible for protecting and caring for the refugees, and eventually life got a little better for them.[46]

Many Christian religious and social organizations sent representatives to help the Hmong with educational and health needs in the refugee camps in Thailand. Traditionally, the Hmong believed in animism, "the way of the spirit," holding that "living and nonliving objects, animals and plants, human beings and nature, all have souls or spirits and are interconnected."[47] Some relief workers converted Hmong to Christianity, and many had already converted from their animist beliefs in Laos. These agencies involved in helping these refugees in the camps included World Vision, Christian and Missionary Alliance (C&MA), Young Women's Christian Association (YWCA), and Catholic Relief Services.[48]

While the Hmong had traditionally been farmers in China, some learned to become nurses or pilots, soldiers, factory workers, and mechanics in Laos. Now in Thailand, their work lives once again changed dramatically. They had always valued their independence and now they were dependent on others to support them and provide food.[49]

While the UNHCR had rules and regulations to protect the refugees and sent millions of dollars to help with health, education, and living facilities, very little help actually reached the Hmong people. Other international organizations also responded to the Hmong refugee crisis and coordinated food, water, housing, and medical supplies. Some Hmong created their own culture with schools and markets. Others got permission and found temporary small jobs outside the camps. They sharpened knives, harvested sugar, and picked coconuts and cotton.[50] Others had relatives in the United States, France, Canada, and Australia who occasionally sent them small sums of money.

Over time, in an effort to keep themselves occupied and to earn some money while in the camps, the women began to make Hmong needlework, called *pa ndau,* which means "flower cloth." Traditionally these story cloths had been only for family use for clothing. They then began to produce their exquisite handiwork in large quantities, hoping to sell it to receive income. Hmong men and boys also began to make the needlework story cloths. The traditional *pa ndau* had abstract designs.

T. Christopher Thao Escapes from Laos

Dr. T. Christopher Thao grew up near Long Cheng in Laos. His parents were subsistence farmers and raised livestock and rice. His father also worked for the government. Thao said that while growing up, everything was a challenge for him. Eventually, he earned a law degree at William Mitchell College of Law and a Ph.D. from Bethel Seminary, both in St. Paul, Minnesota. Currently, he is the pastor at Warren Hmong Alliance Church in Warren, Michigan. "As a young boy, I never imagined I would go through so many changes. I just lived day by day, hoping that something better would come. Difficult times were the war, poverty, and a lack of opportunities."

Back in Laos, Thao left his parents and family to go by bus to Vientiane, the capital. His father sent his younger brother to him with a note, telling Christopher to take him and escape to Thailand. "We hired a boat with a group of Hmong and crossed the Mekong River at night to Thailand. It was about June 16, 1975. My parents and the rest of the family were left behind, except three married sisters who had left days before with their families. I was very frightened and confused. I didn't know what to expect of the future."

Once Thao and his brother arrived in Thailand they went to Nam Phong, a former military site that had been turned into a refugee camp. They found their sisters and other family members. They had been there for about six months when they learned that their parents had gone to another camp, Nong Khai. Since his two older brothers were still in Laos, Thao petitioned the refugee

"Designs go back many centuries. . . . Older women say that in ancient times, *pa ndau* symbolized the knowledge needed for safe passage from this life to the next."[51] The newer pieces told the stories of the Hmong journey. "Tragic in theme yet beautiful in execution, story cloths gain even more significance as part of a worldwide indigenous movement to tell the truth of history through art."[52] In addition to making the story cloths, Hmong also made elaborate jewelry originally from silver but then aluminum. The necklaces became the "second largest source of financial support for many Hmong families."[53]

The women made story cloths to remember their childhood and the war. They sent the tapestries to relatives overseas to sell. Missionaries and refugee officials to move him to Nong Khai to care for his parents and two sisters. They approved and he left for Nong Khai. However, his younger brother remained in Nam Phong with his sisters.

> Nong Khai was a police or military training center. I remember that because of the shooting range that remained. It was a small place, packed with shacks and huts filled with people. The space was fenced with barbed wire. No one could go out. Initially there was no food distribution. People had to buy food from the Thai at the fence. If a family has no money left, they would just wait for others to hand them something to eat. I don't remember how long the people were without food, but sometime later the United Nations came through with food distribution—not enough, but just to sustain life.
>
> We did not have a life in the refugee camp. We wanted to go to school. Our parents had no future. Many people died of sickness and diseases. Every day, the sound of mourning echoed through the camp. It was a scary place. Thai police guards often beat the people who tried to get out to buy food and essentials. Stories of rapes and beatings were an everyday occurrence. The only fun times were Bible studies, soccer games, and volleyball games. Nothing much happened, except death, sickness, and the sounds of mourning. No one wanted to be in the camp. We were there to get away from the Communists. We were afraid to return but had no place to go. Our lives were impaired. That's how we decided to leave and come to America.

aid workers helped them mix "traditional designs with modern colors and materials."[54]

The Christian and Missionary Alliance (C&MA) staff and camp workers encouraged women to make aprons, pillowcases, bedspreads, dish holders, eyeglass cases, and wall hangings to sell to non-Hmong. The designs were Hmong, the objects and color choices were Western "It is still unclear whether this form of Hmong textile was initiated by Hmong or suggested by camp workers or by Hmong relatives who had already fled to the United States."[55]

The Hmong Begin to Leave Camp

When the Thai government initially made an agreement with the Western nations to house the Hmong refugees in camps in their country, they specifically stipulated that it was strictly temporary, not permanent. Therefore, the Hmong began another new, much longer journey.[56] Over a long stretch of thirty years, Hmong refugees emigrated from Thailand and went to the United States, South America, Europe, Oceana, and French Guyana, creating the Hmong diaspora in the West.[57]

However, the Hmong were very weary from their journeys. "The loss and confusion experienced by refugees after separation from their homeland, the unfamiliarity and strangeness of the refugee camps and the uncertainty of the future create an aura of enigma, anxiety and timelessness for the refugee which cannot be overcome as long as they remain in the camps."[58]

In 1951, the United Nations Convention defined a refugee, revising the definition in 1967:

> a person who owing to a well-founded fear of being persecuted for reasons of race, religion, nationality, membership of a particular social group or political opinion, is outside the country of his nationality and is unable or, owing to such fear, is unwilling to avail himself of the protection of that country; or who, not having a nationality and being outside the country of his former habitual residence as a result of such events, is unable or, owing to such fear, is unwilling to return to it.[59]

The Hmong were unquestionably refugees and not just immigrants—people who leave their homeland to go to a new country for educational or economic opportunities. They have continuously feared for their lives—in China, Laos, and Thailand. Furthermore, they have never had a country of their own to which to return.

Some stayed only a few months in camps, while others remained much longer while they waited for family members to join them. The Hmong people's response to their life as refugees in camps varied a great deal. Some could not wait to leave the camps for the United States. Some accepted camp life and stayed for many years until the camps closed and they then had to leave.[60]

Beginning in 1979, more waves of Hmong refugees left Thailand and went to the United States. By the mid-1990s, more than 100,000 Hmong refugees had arrived in the United States.[61] In 2004, the last wave of Hmong refugees left Thailand for the United States.

In the early 1990s, the UNHCR and the Thai government told the refugees that they had to either return to Laos or resettle in a third country. At that time, many Hmong decided to stay at the Wat Tham Krabok Monastery in Thailand, where a Buddhist monk would protect them. When he died in 1999, those Hmong people living in the monastery decided to resettle in the United States.[62]

While some Hmong refugees who went to Thailand may have only lived in camps for a few months, others lived there for twenty or even thirty years. Many had been born in the camps. That was the only life they knew. Some of those young people never had the opportunity to go to school there.

Some Hmong never migrated from Laos to Thailand, and the Thai government repatriated many others back to Laos. Morton Abramowitz, a former US ambassador to Thailand who sits on the board of the International Rescue Committee, and George Rupp, president of the committee, wrote a letter to the *New York Times* criticizing the Thai repatriation (January 7, 2010):

The United Nations High Commissioner for Refugees, the European Union, the United States and leading human rights groups were right to express dismay over the forced return of Hmong to Laos from Thailand. . . . Unfortunately, Thailand did not listen.

But the story is not over. Now that the Hmong returnees are in Laos, everything must be done to ensure that those who deserve refugee status get it.

Most important, the Thai government and United Nations refugee agency must work with Laos to ensure that the returnees receive the appropriate treatment that the Thai government assured the world they would be given, including access to UN and US officials.

The government of Laos should allow a quick departure for the deported refugees who have been approved for US resettlement. The International Rescue Committee stands ready to help recognized refugees resettle in the United States. But what is needed right now is world attention to their plight and that of the other returnees.[63]

Coming to Michigan

Over several centuries of history and always under a cloak of fear, the Hmong people migrated many times from one country to another. They finally left the refugee camps in Thailand beginning in the 1970s to go to the United States and other Western countries. The individuals interviewed whose stories appear here have had many profoundly difficult experiences prior to coming to the United States—adapting to different peoples, cultures, and geography—usually in hostile environments. Throughout their history, the Hmong took few or no tangible belongings with them because they were always running for their lives, often literally on foot. They carried a history deep within filled with obstacles, warfare, persecution, death, confusion, pain, and suffering. As a people, individually and collectively, they have overcome numerous barriers on their long journey to resettle in Michigan. Yet they are amazingly resilient. Coming to America, and specifically Michigan, they have found a home where "they could belong and be free."[64]

While resettling in Michigan, the Hmong have had to abandon the familiar and cope with many new challenges, including a different culture, language, work, school, customs, industry, technology, communications, economics, religion, culture, race, and environment. Perhaps their numerous migration experiences and profound capacity to adapt to new situations have ironically made them strong and enduring. [65] As a people the Hmong were extremely motivated not only to leave the camps, but also to seek an education and work in a new homeland so they could become free, productive citizens. "The tension created by the persistence of old ways adapting to a new environment is one that is conquered by survivors. With a reputation for surviving tough times, the Hmong are coping better than many other immigrant groups." [66]

As the main international coordinating agency, the United Nations High Commissioner for Refugees (UNHCR) helps refugees move from hostile environments to resettle in new safe homes in the United States and other countries around the world. Since the refugee camps in Thailand were only a temporary home for the Hmong, the UNHCR mobilized efforts to work together with international volunteer organizations to transport the Hmong to such faraway lands as the United States, France, and Australia.

The UNHCR works with governments to identify refugees who desperately need help to resettle. They include those who face threats of repatriation or threats by the country of first asylum. Others were those who have disabilities or health problems.[67] Sadly, many Hmong families initially were divided and sent to different countries. [68] In the chaos of migrating, at least they knew that in America, Communists would not kill them and their children could attend school, which would ultimately provide opportunities. [69]

Resettlement is a complex process. "It is a powerful tool of protection for individual refugees, a means to secure other rights, a durable solution for those who cannot go home or integrate in the country of first asylum, and a means by which states can share the responsibility for refugees with overburdened host countries and by doing so bolster their commitment to providing first asylum. . . . Resettlement is also used to enable refugees to get vital medical treatment not available to them in the country of first asylum."[70] In the United States, however, the Hmong encountered bureaucratic and social pitfalls

> The Hmong people's traditional values of family, kin, and clan welfare were in direct and continuous conflict with the values of the American social welfare system as well as the American ideologies of independence and self-determination. . . . The accelerated lifestyle of the United States has resulted in turmoil, difficulties, and crises for a people who did not possess the necessary skills to successfully deal with the changes.[71]

The Hmong faced these major challenges when they came to Michigan beginning in the mid-1970s: a new culture, society, customs, politics, religion, and recreation. Many had never used electricity or indoor plumbing.

Religious and Community Organizations and Sponsors

Religious and community volunteer organizations worked with the refugees in the Thailand camps and then continued their transition to America, and more specifically to California and the Midwest—Minnesota, Wisconsin, and Michigan. Churches, non-Hmong individuals, or Hmong refugees sponsored each of the Hmong individuals or families who are portrayed in this book. These community organizations "see the care of resettling refugees as part of their core mandate." [72] Initial refugees then became sponsors for relatives and friends. [73] "By 1985, seventy-two Hmong communities had been established in the United States, ranging in size from less than one hundred to more than ten thousand people." [74]

The first Hmong refugees who came to the United States in the mid-1970s went to both urban and rural areas. Prior to 1975, Hmong people did not live in the United States except for a few graduate students who had come because of their alliance with American military or with humanitarian personnel during the war years. "Within a short period of time, the refugees were exposed to many environments across the country and thus were able to compare and contrast different geographical locations." [75]

Hmong refugees often did not remain in the communities where they initially settled. Often they migrated to other communities where they had relatives and a larger Hmong community. They also moved for better jobs, education, welfare benefits, and a warmer climate, both in terms of the weather and the community's acceptance of them. Initially, they had little opportunity to choose the original host community, but eventually had a greater opportunity to determine the best community based on their particular, individual preferences. [76] Some American sponsors appreciated and supported the Hmong people's decisions to move from their original communities, while others did not. [77]

In the *Frankenmuth News* (March 4, 2009), journalist Susan McInerney wrote about the Hang family, who originally came to Richville, Michigan, as refugees from Laos. Lutherans had sponsored many Hmong refugees who moved to Alaska, Michigan, Wisconsin, California, and Minnesota. Reverends William Schoenow and Victor Spiekerman, who were pastors at St. Michaels in Richville, learned about the refugees' plight through the US Department of State and wanted to help. "Many gracious and kindhearted residents opened their homes and their pocketbooks to make the Hang's transition possible," according to Hmong pastor Lang Yang of Richville, who himself left a Thai refugee camp at age eleven.[78] Over time, Tru Hang continued the missionary spirit by helping financially to sponsor the immigration of five other Hmong families to the United States.

When I talked with Hmong Americans in Michigan, several said that since the economy was so poor in the first decade of the twenty-first century, many of their friends and relatives moved to the southern states to start chicken farms, including Arkansas, North Carolina, Georgia, Florida, and Oklahoma. They went into the chicken business because they were familiar with raising chickens back in Laos. T. Christopher Thao, pastor of the Warren Hmong Alliance Church, said,

> The city networks, social networking, adult education, the social safety net, like welfare and the economic factors and the support from churches and non-profit organizations really helped maintain and stabilize the community. For example, Lutheran Social Services, Catholic Services, refugee resettlement people brought people to the hospital. These are very important factors to maintain stability here besides employment.

According to the Office of Refugee Resettlement (ORR), US Department of Health and Human Services, report to Congress, "The ability to speak English is one of the most important factors influencing the economic self-sufficiency of refugees. . . . Overall, the findings from ORR's 2006 survey indicate that the newly resettled Hmong refugees faced significant problems upon arrival in the U.S., especially the female members of this group. They have, however, made significant strides in achieving independence."[79]

In an interview (2010), Judi Harris, director of refugee services for St. Vincent Catholic Services in Lansing, said:

> Resettlement agencies help refugees make the transition from the country in which they live by preparing them for their trip and initial orientation   .

T. Christopher Thao Travels to the United States

T. Christopher Thao's journey to the United States is a good example of Hmong Americans who did not remain in the community of sponsorship. His story is an interesting one. While family and friends did not find his original sponsor, he eventually moved closer to family.

Thao was young and longed to get out of the refugee camp and make a living. When the opportunity arose for him to go overseas, he was glad. He left Nong Khai on August 25, 1976, for Bangkok and then, on September 3, 1976, left Bangkok for the United States. "My parents were afraid for me, but there's no life in the refugee camps, so they let me come. I was eighteen when I made the decision."

Thao and his brothers had been students in Laos, but there was no schooling in the refugee camps, no life, no future without education. It was hard for their parents. "They were not sure what the future would bring and didn't see a future in another country. Their minds, their frame of reference was always back home in Laos. My father said, 'You are the renegade son, always pushing the issue. I won't let your older and your younger brothers go. You are so insistent. You can go on your own.' My parents wanted to wait a couple of years. But, for us, our lives were impaired. That's how we decided to leave for America."

Thao said he had studied English and had conversations with Americans in Laos and camps in Thailand, as well as missionaries who worked with him so he could get a sense of what America was like. He also saw pictures of American cities.

As children growing up, you still have this curiosity about adventure that we want to go to cities and places you want to see. So I had that within me and the prospect of my continuing my education. I wanted to come. I talked to a French man and woman about educational opportunities in France who said the best I could do with the language is go to trade school. However, American missionaries said, "You can go to school at whatever age you want to, so America became the land, the Promised Land. I use some biblical language to describe this experience for me. The American Funds for Czechoslovakian Refugees in New York City sponsored me to that little city of Jasper, Arkansas.

I landed in Seattle in the morning, so I didn't see much of Seattle. I was driven from the airport to a motel to stay and sleep in the day and waited for the next day to fly to the Ozarks. I was leaving Seattle, so I could only see the skyscrapers from where I was, and I saw the beauty of the city and it was a wonderful sight. A view of the ocean was beautiful. But once I got into the plane, they put me in the window seat. I could see the beauty of the whole city. It was breathtaking at that time. Highways crisscrossing one another. That was wonderful, a very special treat.

Thao then went to Harrison, Arkansas, in the Ozark Mountains. He just saw farmland and forests on his flight on a clear day in September. When the plane landed, he stepped out, walked into the waiting area, and met his sponsor, Margaret, who was alone to greet him. He went to high school there. Margaret wanted Thao to finish the year before he moved on, but he was so homesick.

I didn't know if I could live in that depressing setting with the wild cat I had seen and her twenty or so domestic cats. She had a pond and I fed the fish. Those were pretty much the activities that I did—live with the cats, go to the pond and feed the fish, and come back into her little mobile home. I was very homesick and lonely in Jasper. I didn't know if I could tolerate life any longer there. I had no relatives, friends, or a Hmong community. I moved to Pennsylvania and then New York to pursue my education and work. Margaret was

and adjustment to their new homeland. Once the refugees arrive in the United States, the agencies help them communicate with state and local authorities for employment and welfare, find clean housing, furniture, food, clothing, refer them to appropriate health programs, assist them to apply for Social Security cards, help them register their children for school and provide transportation for job interviews and training. The goal of these agencies is to help the refugees become self-sufficient.

Harris explained that Catholic Social Service agencies strongly believe that such a humanitarian response and investment with refugees to save lives improves our community as a whole and improves our relationships as well as our economy. "Over half of Michigan immigrants, or 64.4 percent, are heartbroken to say good-bye to me, and I could sense her brokenness. She did show some anger, maybe because her dream for me was not fulfilled. I did not finish school year there. She had no way to [send] me to my people in a way that would shield my emotional problem at the time. As she was taking me to the bus station, she did not talk a lot. I could see the expression on her face.

Thao left Jasper to stay with cousins in Philadelphia, then went to New York to work at a resort in the Pocono Mountains, and then went to college. He returned to Philadelphia to prepare for his parents' arrival. The Baptist church sponsored them. They then moved to Minnesota, and eventually he moved to California and then Michigan.

Many years later, Thao went back to Jasper on a memory trip. Margaret had died; a neighbor of hers told him

Peggy was supposed to have me as the son she never had. She had past issues with the law, had run away and settled in the Arkansas woods to find peace and tranquility. Margaret might have felt in her own life that she really experienced the trauma of running away, when she heard about the trauma of refugees from Southeast Asia. It might have been an emotional attachment to the trauma that the refugees have run away from their homeland—maybe motivated her. So there may be a multitude of reasons, of motivators.

of working age (eighteen to fifty-four) [in 2010], compared with 50.8 percent of the nonimmigrant population in 2008. This is a critical factor as a large portion of the state is nearing retirement."

Furthermore, she said, "When considering the workforce and exodus from Michigan, who is left to work, produce, consume, and pay taxes? Along with general population infusion, necessary for a healthy economy, refugees bring youth, vitality, skills, and diversity."

According to Harris, federal funding for cities often decreases if the population drops below 100,000; Lansing currently has about 115,000 people. Refugees contribute about 250 new students to the Lansing School District annually that increase funding to the district; buy and rent homes in inner-city neighborhoods and make these neighborhoods family friendly; create new small businesses including stores and restaurants; and tend to stay in the city and generate taxes.

Patricia Hepp, former director of refugee resettlement for St. Vincent Catholic Charities (STVCC) in Lansing, Michigan, talked about her memories and challenges when she worked with the Hmong refugees. She said that the role of the organization was to serve these people, not to proselytize them.

Hepp had never heard of the Hmong before she started working with them. "My job was so exciting, the best job I could have ever had—to educate populations, to have people on our staff that the community respected. We had more than one staff person who was Hmong American."

> I took the early Hmong arrivals to their new homes myself. People were not available to help in the community, and at the time, there was very little orientation for the refugees. Now there's much better orientation. I opened the freezer filled with frozen food, but then realized that they did not even know what ice was. I wondered, "What were they thinking?" Not, "What was *I* thinking? I wonder how they survived.
>
> The first arrivals had a very difficult time. We had to get the kids to school. They have to get their health checked. The adults have to have employment. They have to learn English. It takes a community to help. The agency can't do all of it alone. I think the program was so successful in the Lansing area with the Hmong because it was not a huge group. We did not have the problems with the gangs and people on welfare.
>
> One of the best employers of the Hmong Americans is Quality Dairy. The Hmong make all the donuts here. Meijer is also one of the best employers. They really want to welcome the strangers. A large majority are homeowners. Many of the next generation are getting an education. That is the key here.

Hepp talked about the Hmong people's initial cultural challenges as they began to resettle in the greater Lansing area. She was particularly pleased with the Greater Lansing community's positive and unbelievably accepting response to their new neighbors. "It only works because so many things were in place. The school system was quite proud of their work." Sometimes, she was overwhelmed by the low level of skills and education some of the refugees had. But she saw how much progress they made.

The American dream is possible! People can do it. They did it and they still do it. Those who just stayed with their families, their nationality group and their secure place and did not want to venture out took a long time to adjust. We can only hope that the second generation will become successful. People become refugees not for themselves. It's for the kids.

Hepp shared a couple of stories of about what she called "cultural clashes" that exemplified the challenges of adapting to a new culture. She spoke of a group that had a worm business. They went out at night with flashlights on their heads looking for worms in people's backyards and in cemeteries. They then sold the worms—so much per coffee can—to a man who would then sell them in Ohio to people for fishing.

"The Hmong did not understand personal property." she said. "You can't just go into someone's yard. I would get a call. 'Your people were out there. I saw them eating those worms. You can't believe how they ate those worms.' But nobody was eating the worms. I always thought what if the truck driver had an accident and then there would be all these worms on the road!"

Hepp also told a story about the time a young fellow saw a "suitable female" he thought he wanted. Apparently, the Hmong have a custom of "kidnapping the potential bride." "He and his friends went to kidnap the young woman at McDonalds, where she was working. The screams went on. That particular time the police came to ask me what was going on. They had tried to intervene, but they had no idea what was going on. They backed off. The police told me that I had to start educating them. They told me, 'This can't go on' and I must stop it."

In 1983, C. Kurt Dewhurst, former director of the Museum at Michigan State University, and Marsha MacDowell, curator of folk arts at the same museum, documented some of the earliest information about the Hmong refugees who came to the Greater Lansing area. Since that time, much has changed in the Hmong community.

In October 1976, the first Hmong refugees, Teng Vang and two of his younger cousins, and Tong Her and a few members of his family settled in Grand Ledge, Michigan. Over the next two years, more Hmong refugees began to come. Several churches provided support to these families—in particular St. Michael's in Grand Ledge; Our Savior Lutheran Church, East Lansing; and All Saints Episcopal Church in East Lansing, and a Refugee

Services Office was established by Catholic Social Services. The Hmong community grew to 500. Other Hmong refugees went to Saginaw, Detroit, Pontiac, and briefly the Thumb area.

> These communities are all tightly connected by clans, organizational leadership, ritual observance, and social intercourse. . . . In Lansing, the Hmong existence has been marked by employment at places such as the Wohlert Corporation, Leon's foods, and the Quality Dairy Bakery; participation in community garden projects behind the Marshall Street Armory and our Savior Lutheran Church; the staging of cultural shows at churches, schools, and New Years' parties; and the formation of soccer teams. Rock bands have also been formed by groups of primarily young Hmong who have rather quickly intertwined Western and Indochinese musical traditions in producing a unique sound. These bands vie for trophies at competitions held at New Years' parties and other Hmong events in Michigan. In the past year, Lansing Hmong have even joined with other Lansing area Indochinese in establishing an Indochinese Center where classes, meetings and special events regularly take place. [80]

Through the auspices of Catholic Social Services, St. Michael Parish in Grand Ledge became involved in resettling and supporting Southeast Asian refugees following the collapse of the American-supported governments in Laos and later in Vietnam. St. Michael in Grand Ledge sponsored Tong Her, his wife Mae Lou, and their children.

When the US federal government allowed these refugees to enter this country, it required that an organization sponsor them that would commit to providing as many resources as possible to help them make the transition to life in America.

Chris and Mary Dancisak were cochairs of the sponsorship committee for St. Michael Church in Grand Ledge. They worked with Betty Marsh, another parishioner, who took responsibility for daily interaction with Tong Her and his wife. They had first helped settle a Vietnamese family sponsored by the church. At the time, Chris worked for the Michigan House of Representatives and Mary taught at St. Michaels. Their primary role was to assist Tong in the search for a job, help the Her family find housing, and help them adapt to our culture.

Chris explained how and why he decided to cosponsor this committee to help settle refugees from Southeast Asia.

> I became involved because I was antiwar in that period, and some of the consequences of the Vietnam conflict at the end of it were a lot of people were displaced because they trusted America and were basically run out of their country with the threat of their lives hanging over them. I felt we had a moral responsibility to do all we could to help them resettle and adapt to culture as the result of the faith that they put into our government and its actions.

The Dancisaks, with Betty Marsh and the pastor of the church, went as a delegation to greet the Her family when they arrived at the Lansing airport.

> They arrived in the evening. It was dark, snowy, and rainy a mixture of snowy rain. They came off the plane with two or three children. One of them had been born in the refugee camp in Thailand and was under a year old. Mae Lou was holding the baby. I think we held a sign that said the "Her Family." The baby was wrapped in dishrags that the flight attendant must have given them. They had run out of diapers. The plane ride was twenty-seven hours from Thailand to Lansing. A pretty memorable experience!

Tong could speak more than passable English because he had worked with the American military. His wife could not speak any English.

> It was certainly a moving experience that I have never forgotten. What these people had gone through not only that day but also throughout their lives was unbelievable! The transition that they were now being forced to make was amazing. They had been born in a completely alien society.

The church still had a house available that Vietnamese refugees had previously used. Chris and his wife helped settle the Hers in their new home. They wanted them to become familiar with toilets. "They were certainly not used to things we considered modern necessities." Shortly after that, we moved them into a different, smaller home.

Chris and Mary spent time with the Hers on a regular basis. They tried to help them acclimate to the society. Chris remembers that the family was overwhelmed when the Dancisaks took them to Meijer.

> We took them grocery shopping, which was another unique experience. They were coming from a refugee camp in Thailand where they did not even have the necessities. Then they came to America and had this relatively nice home—dry and warm. Then they go from that environment into a modern automobile. They go to a grocery store that has just about anything that you think you would ever want. Meijer has clothes, toys, and everything else. You can just imagine what these folks were thinking! I can't imagine! But I do know it was an interesting experience because all of a sudden they were exposed to all this.

The Dancisaks tried to help the Hers better understand what kinds of foods they should be looking for when they went to grocery store, so they would eat properly and not spend money needlessly. They explained the different meats and learned quite quickly that the mainstay of their diet was chicken and rice. They tried to help them stretch their money and thought that orange juice would be a good option for them but that it would be expensive. As an alternative, Chris and Mary introduced the Hers to Tang—the orange juice concentrate used by the astronauts.

> We found out humorously that it probably was not the smartest thing we did because every time we went to visit them, they brought out little trays with Tang in little cups instead of tea! It wasn't cold. It was lukewarm Tang. It came back to haunt us!

The Hers got accustomed to cooking things. The family had not learned that in the United States food was generally served warmed or hot. Chris said that there was rarely a time that they would visit that there would not be a meal of lukewarm chicken. "I don't know if that was a cultural thing or if they hadn't gotten acclimated. They were not used to refrigeration or that you can warm things up."

Betty Marsh found Tong Her a job working for a local car dealership washing cars. Tong was an extremely hard worker. It was during a period

Chue Kue Moves to Michigan

When I left Thailand, I came straight to Detroit, Michigan. I was very happy to leave the camp because there was no life there. I was very happy that I would finally reunite with all my aunties and uncles. All my cousins came to Philly first, and then moved to Michigan. My cousin was the one that helped look for a sponsor for my family. The Lutherans were our sponsor. I was very happy to leave Thailand and anxious to meet my family. I was clueless how my new home would look like.

Most people knew that we are jungle people because we lived on the high mountain. When we first got to the States my sponsor took us for shopping, and we bought some oranges. When we got home, I took an orange, peeled it, and shared it with the family. My sponsor said, "I thought you are going to eat the whole orange without peeling it because you are jungle people." I smiled and told her that we live in a tropical climate country, and we grow many different kinds of fruits. I said that we lived in the city, and we have doctors, nurses, and pilots.

that jobs were pretty easy to come by, compared to what immigrants might face today unless they are highly educated.

Chris said that Tong had been involved with the American military and other Americans back in Laos, and Chris thought that made it easier for him to make the transition. "He was very intelligent. He grasped things very quickly in the transition, which was a major advantage for him and his family—the exposure to things American even though he had not been exposed to them directly. The Hers had a number of children. They were Catholic before they came here. There was the desire to teach them the rhythm method. I'm not sure they ever got that. They desired to repopulate. My understanding is that the family has since moved to California."

Some refugees such as Chue Kue had amusing recollections of their early experiences with their sponsors.

Adapting to Michigan

While the Hmong refugees have faced major challenges and difficulties adapting to Michigan, several significant factors have helped them survive and thrive. They have a tremendous ability and desire to preserve their culture and family that strengthens them individually and collectively. They have maintained connections with extended family within Michigan, the United States, and overseas. Vegetable gardening has helped some of the Michigan residents, particularly the elderly, to maintain ties with their past life in Laos, where they were predominately farmers. This has helped them stabilize their lives as they adapt to a radically different culture and society. Raising chickens and fishing has also helped them connect with the past.

As Hmong Americans have pursued a path to self-sufficiency for themselves and their children, they have found jobs in factories, the health care industry, and education. Many in Michigan have also gone into the restaurant business. They preserve traditions by celebrating the New Year and playing sports and maintain a balance between their past and contemporary life. Those who have adapted more easily appear to have achieved a balance between the old and the new, individually and collectively.

Hmong Americans are hearty, resilient, hard workers who have persevered and continue to face a multitude of challenges in their complicated lives. The Hmong are "quintessential multitaskers"—while they carry heavy memories from the past, they simultaneously manage their ongoing daily realities and frustrations to make their lives and their children's lives more comfortable and productive.

How do they digest such loss and begin to absorb those dramatically different experiences in such radically foreign environments under profoundly difficult circumstances within a relatively short time and simultaneously move their lives forward? How do they cope with the pain of having lost so many loved ones through such brutality—drowning? murder? starvation? How do they tolerate the temporary or permanent loss of and separation from extended family? How do they build new relationships with yet another people so unfamiliar to them? How do they maintain a semblance of stability when their lives have been in perpetual motion through little choice of their own? How do they manage with nothing to help them—no personal, tangible old stuff, historic documents, or family photographs to remind them of their past?

Hmong refugees came as children, teenagers, single adults, and married couples with their children and elderly grandparents to the United States. Once in Michigan, they no longer had to flee for their lives, fight in a war, or live in a brutal refugee camp with no freedom and little to do. After an initial orientation and help from family or from non-Hmong sponsors, churches, and the government, how did they establish themselves, become self-sufficient, and deal with freedom and opportunities that they or their ancestors had never experienced? For the first time in their lives, the Hmong have found themselves in a country with a government and society that provide opportunities for self-determination, to pursue their education, work, and still allow them the freedom to preserve Hmong culture and family ties.

Many researchers have written about the Hmong people's challenge adapting to their new homes in the United States. Cathleen Jo Faruque has written that the Hmong people have accepted the challenge of adapting while simultaneously maintaining their unique identity.[81] Dewhurst and MacDowell describe the mixed cultural practices the Hmong have developed:

> Among the changes these Hmong have undergone are the acquisition of
> a new language, the employment of men and women in new occupations,

the adoption of a new religion, shifts in male and female or youth and age roles, and the use of new apparel. No longer do the men fight wars or the women farm; no more do the young look solely to their elders to obtain knowledge; no longer do women work only in the home. When an illness occurs, the shaman may be consulted before or after visiting an M.D.; when a child is born the baptism rites may be followed with naming parties; and when a young couple marries, tuxedos and traditional clothes may be intermixed. The old traditions shift, change, adapt and are transformed, but they haven't died.[82]

Hmong strengths are multifaceted, which helped them survive when they made the transition from subsistence agriculture in Laos to refugee camps in Thailand and finally to life in a capitalist society. They are extremely self-sufficient, maintain strong bonds with their relatives, and feel tremendous loyalty and responsibility to help them. Because of their past difficulties, they have great reservoirs of resilience and make the best of opportunities to contribute positively to their new homeland.[83]

It would be unrealistic, however, to present an image of their adaptation to the United States as always easy, smooth, and successful. They confront immense challenges in their new life—language, education, work, religion, race, and ethnicity. The move from a rural society to a high-technology one, with few skills, was a particularly difficult adaptation.[84] Yet today first-generation Hmong Americans are pursuing higher education and entering the job force as professionals in the health care, education, and business worlds.

English professor Sheng-Mei Ma at Michigan State University writes about the importance of individual feelings among Hmong refugees and the health problems some have had experienced as a consequence of their past trauma. Some of the men suffered from::

The Sudden Unexpected Nocturnal Death Syndrome (SUNDS), which in the 1970s and 1980s mysteriously struck Hmong and other Southeast Asian male refugees in their sleep. Some survivors claimed an attack . . . on their chests, pressing the air out of their lungs. Western doctors could do no more than attribute the cases to cardiac arrest in otherwise perfectly healthy men, a great number of whom reported depression and ill-adjustment to the United States.[85]

Unfortunately, some teenagers of Hmong origin have become involved in gangs and violence. This has contributed to stereotyping Hmong Americans by people who have little or no comprehension about the group as a whole. Most views have come from negative news reports: the teenagers and men charged with raping four Hmong Michigan girls in Wisconsin, the Hmong hunter in Wisconsin accused of killing several other hunters, and stories of gang violence in Detroit.[86] This is why we need to understand these people outside of the sensational negative news reports. Indeed, the Hmong people fought for the United States in the war in Laos and lost 35,000 of their own people—more than half as many as Americans who died in the Vietnam War. They are extremely loyal to the United States and have made significant contributions to this country.[87]

An Associated Press report from St. Paul, Minnesota, describes General Vang Pao's new fight against gang violence in the United States:

> He told parents to encourage their children to study harder and to make sure they regularly attend school. He also said Hmong parents should concentrate more on building strong families.
>
> Pao said he has witnessed the effects of gang-related violence in the Hmong community in California, Colorado, and Michigan. He attributed much of the rise in gang violence to the reluctance of parents to report their children who may be involved in gangs to police, or elders in community organizations.[88]

Interestingly, Clint Eastwood filmed a major movie, *Gran Torino*, in metro Detroit, including Highland Park, Center Line, Warren, Royal Oak, and Gross Pointe Park. The movie addressed issues of discrimination and ethnic stereotyping and gave visibility to an ethnic population little known to most people. Clint Eastwood wanted to have real Hmong Americans play the roles of Hmong characters and did not want professional actors from other Asian or Asian American ethnic groups. He also hired Hmong American crew, production assistants, consultants, and extras.[89]

> The original story of curmudgeonly widower Walt Kowalski finding an unexpected degree of kinship with the Hmong community was set in Min-

neapolis, but director Clint Eastwood felt Kowalski's past as an auto worker
made the Motor City itself, Detroit the ideal backdrop.

Detroit has been hit hard by the decline of the car industry, but isn't
taking the setback lying down. A new tax incentive package offered to film
productions by the state of Michigan clinched the deal, and *Gran Torino*
became the first film to benefit. With the production crew spending more
than $10 million in town during the 33-day shoot, well, everybody's happy.[90]

Two of the people interviewed for this book, coincidentally, were actors in
the movie. Tru Hang played the grandfather in the house next door to Walt
Kowalski. Maykao Lytongpao played the role of one of the aunties. Other
Michigan residents of Hmong origin also performed in the movie, including
"Sue," the main star, Ahney Her, when she was sixteen years old. She has
since graduated from Sexton High School in Lansing and gone on to attend
Michigan State University.

An article appeared in the *Lansing City Pulse* based on Tim Barron's interview on WQTX with Ahney Her. Ahney said that she met Clint Eastwood on
the first day of the shooting. "I had no idea what I was doing, but when I met
him, he was very kind. I knew he was a big, important guy, but I didn't know
how big and important. He sent a very nice and comfortable vibe." When
Ahney got the part, she said, "I was actually quite calm. It didn't hit me until
a couple weeks later that I was in such a big movie."[91]

Demographics of Hmong Americans in Michigan

How many Hmong Americans live in the United States? How many of
them live in Michigan and where? According to the US 2010 census data,
306,738,422 people live in the United States. Of those, 260,073 are Hmong
Americans. The number of persons of Hmong descent has grown in the past
three decades. In 1990, 94,439 persons of Hmong origin lived in the United
States. By 2000, the population jumped to 186,310. From 1990 to 2010, the
Hmong American population increased by 175 percent. The Hmong population is quite young. Among Asian American ethnic groups, "only the Hmong
and Japanese possess an American-born population outnumbering the
foreign-born population."[92]

The greatest number of Hmong Americans in the Midwest reside in Minnesota, Wisconsin, and then Michigan. As of 2010, the largest number of Hmong in the United States, 126,713 (just less than 49 percent), live in the Midwest.[93]

The US 2010 census data report 9,883,640 people live in Michigan. Of those, 5,924 are of Hmong descent. Presumably, because of tough economic times in Michigan when Hmong Americans migrated south, this figure represents a decrease of 10 percent from 2000, when 5,988 Hmong Americans lived in Michigan. However, back in 1990, 2,304 persons of Hmong origin lived in Michigan. Overall, the Hmong American population increased 157 percent from 1990 to 2010.

The largest concentration of Hmong Americans in Michigan is in the Detroit-Wayne-Livonia area, including Pontiac, Warren, and Sterling Heights as well. Many also live east of the Coleman Young Airport close to Conner Avenue, Gratiot Avenue, and McNichols Avenue (4,190). The second largest Hmong American community in Michigan lives in the Lansing–East Lansing area (958).[94]

Those who live in the northern Detroit area east of the Coleman Young Airport often attend social activities at Osborn High School. In December 1999 Osborn had 1,900 students. During that year, 250 of them were Hmong American, and the boys' volleyball team was 95 percent Hmong American.[95]

Michelle Lin, the coordinator of the Detroit Asian Youth (DAY) Project remarks, "They think of themselves as Hmong. They think of themselves as Asian. 'Asian-American' is something more intangible that they can't really grasp. The DAY Project takes high school students out of their neighborhoods and into Detroit's wider-ranging cultural life. The goal of the DAY Project is to develop leadership skills and raise awareness of social justice issues by understanding Detroit and its Asian-American community."[96] One Hmong American participant in the DAY Project, Dia ShiaYang, "believes that while she looks at Detroit history from a distance and sees it as traumatic, she also sees herself as part of that history that's unfolding."[97]

Another participant in the DAY Project of Hmong descent, Mai Ka Yeng Moua, who was born in Thailand, graduated from Osborn High School in 2006. "Despite the hardship of her life in Detroit, Moua believes she's better off for the experience. 'I wasn't given everything handed down to me. I had to make my way through it. It gave me a sense of who I am. It made me appreciate my life . . . and my community more.'"[98]

Many of those who live in the Detroit and Lansing areas have relatives in other communities throughout Michigan—such as Owosso, Mt. Pleasant, Jackson, Battle Creek, and 'Up North' in Petoskey, Traverse City, and Marquette (see appendix 1). Initially churches and their congregants sponsored Hmong refugees to Michigan; those newcomers, in turn, often sponsored newer arrivals to come to Michigan. They then tried to help their relatives and friends get on their feet. Some settled near their sponsoring families, while others decided to move to other Michigan communities.

Family Connections

Family and specifically extended family is extremely important to Michigan residents of Hmong descent. They work hard to maintain relationships with relatives not only within Michigan, but elsewhere in the United States and overseas.

> Historically, the Hmong male has held the leadership roles for both home and community, as well as having the primary responsibility for raising sons. Hmong women remain silent in discussions and matters of governance within the clan. Hmong women are primarily responsible for childbirth, tending to the home, assisting in the fields, and teaching the traditions of the Hmong people to the children. Recent exposure to the United States and its culture, education for the Hmong, especially for females, and new opportunities for younger Hmong people has [*sic*] resulted in challenges both to the roles of family and the politics of the clan.[99]

Some Hmong Americans who have been living in the United States for more than thirty years, such as Ying Xiong, former owner of the Thai Kitchen in East Lansing, return to Laos to visit extended family who still live there. Going back to Laos and Thailand to visit with relatives and old friends who remained behind is a key element that strengthens them not only as extended families but as a nuclear family and as individuals.

Nghia Tran, a Vietnamese-American health coordinator at St. Vincent

Catholic Charities in Lansing, has worked for more than twenty years with refugees from all over the world. In a recent interview, he said that of all the people who have come to the Lansing area, the Hmong are the only ones who always consult with families and friends before trusting an outsider from a social service or government agency.

The Hmong adapted to a new life while still maintaining their ethnic bonds. As they began to rebuild their lives, some clung to shamanism while others became Christians. They began to meet at people's homes, creating self-help groups to talk about the challenges they were experiencing trying to adapt to their new environment and society. Simultaneously, they held workshops to teach those who wanted to learn how to conduct traditional rituals.[100]

Vegetable Gardening, Raising Chickens, and Fishing

Another way in which Hmong people stay connected with their past and simultaneously adapt to their new life in a healing, nurturing way is through vegetable and herb gardening. In this way, they remain connected with the land. As mentioned earlier, the Hmong were slash-and-burn farmers in Laos, as were their ancestors back in China. Women are the primary vegetable gardeners in the family, and many Hmong people have vegetable gardens at their homes.[101]

In the middle of winter after a huge snowstorm, I interviewed Tru Hang and his son, Fu, at their home in Fenton, Michigan. Tru's wife, Li, had prepared an elaborate, traditional, delicious Hmong meal with about eight different entrées. Li apologized for not having had more time to prepare, as the meal would have been even better! The Hang family said a prayer before the meal and graciously thanked me for coming to help them share their story. They understood and appreciated the book's purpose.

One of the dishes Li made was a green, leafy vegetable, similar to spinach, called *gai choy*. She had grown it the previous summer in her garden, and then frozen it for the winter. Fu explained that most Asian vegetable and fruit stores in Michigan carry it in many variations; it is also known as Chinese mustard greens. Hmong American women typically have vegetable gardens in their yard or through community garden projects in Michigan so that their family can eat the vegetables year round.

From left to right: Fu Hang, Fu's nephew, Tru Hang, and Li Hang at lunch in their home. Photo by the author.

Fu said, "We don't have any formal recipes per say, but it's pretty much stir-fry any vegetables with meat, vegetable soup with or without meat. It's pretty simple. We have adopted cuisine from other cooking, like Laotian, Thai, and Vietnamese."

> Gardening connects Hmong women to their past, their traditional chores in Laos, and provides a sense of worth for them now that they are in the United States. . . . The act of gardening and the garden site themselves provide a space for reflexivity in which memories of the home country are arranged and refitted into new patterns of life in the United States.[102]

Not only do the Hmong women raise vegetables for their own family consumption but they also often sell them at farmers' markets, which have proliferated throughout the United States. From 1994 to 2004, according to the United States Department of Agriculture (USDA) AMS Farmer Market facts, farmer markets have grown by 111 percent.[103]

In the Greater Lansing area, the Self-Help Garden Project began in 1983 as part of the Greater Lansing Food Bank, a nonprofit organization that provides emergency food to individuals and families in Ingham, Eaton, and Clinton counties. The Garden Project promotes a healthy food system and encourages people to grow home and community gardens.

> The Project works to grow healthy food and cultivated connections with the goal of helping create a healthier food system in the Greater Lansing area. It helps provide training, resources and technical support to local groups facilitating the start of eleven new community gardens in 2011. It assists home and community gardeners in Ingham, Eaton and Clinton counties to grow and preserve their own fresh vegetables and provides access to land, seeds, plants, tools and more to about 80 community gardens. They also organize a gleaning program with volunteers to harvest surplus produced from the area farms, totaling around 250,000 pounds a year.[104]

In 1987, journalist Rhonda Sewell interviewed the project director, Paul Brink. He said, "The Hmong are excellent gardeners. It's neat going out there (to the gardens). It's like seeing artists at work."[105]

More recently in 2012, Anne Raucher, director of the Garden Project, said, "The gardens are the hub of the community for people to catch up with other folks. Many refugees including the Bhutanese, Burmese, Hmong and others rent plots to garden about twenty-five feet by twenty-five feet. They used to be rent-free. Now the Garden Project charges five dollars a plot. Some people rent more than one plot in more than one location. Sometimes whole families work in the gardens."[106]

According to the Garden Project's annual report for 2011, "A healthy food system provides all community members—especially limited resource residents including children and the elderly—with opportunities to acquire easily accessible and affordable nutritious food, produced locally and using environmentally sound practices."[107] Over 7,500 people involved in this project grew vegetables valued at an estimated $600,000. This was the result of more than ninety community gardens and three hundred home gardens. Nurseries, individuals, and groups donated over 35,000 plant starts and 5,300 seed packages. More than 5,000 wheelbarrow loads of compost were delivered to local gardens.

In the *Spartan Online Newsroom*, a project of Michigan State University's School of Journalism, students wrote:

Tong Vue Gardens in Michigan

Christine Xiong's maternal grandmother is Tong Vue, who is also Lian Xiong's mother and seventy-four years old. Before she came to America, she said she was excited. "It couldn't be worse than what we experienced. So this was the hope."

Tong Vue has participated for many years in the Self-Help Garden Project in Lansing. While she understands spoken English, she still has difficulties speaking the language, so Christine translated for her while we stood in one of her rented plots of land in a huge field near the Lansing airport. She had a particularly lovely, cheerful demeanor. It was clear that she really loves to garden and finds it very satisfying.

Tong Vue works at many of the gardens in the area, often for twelve hours a day. She drives a minivan and takes her cell phone with her. Her son checks up on her either by stopping by to see her working in one of the fields or calling her. Christine said that their whole family, all ten of them, use to work in the garden plots. Tong Vue gets seeds from the Garden Project. She grows lettuce, cilantro, onions, squash, cucumbers, peppers, eggplants, melons, lemongrass, mint, and tomatoes. She uses strings of videotape around her garden to keep out the deer. Sometimes she sells her produce at the local vegetable markets or at the Oriental Market. She also freezes many of her vegetables for the winter months.

She said, "I like to exercise in the garden. If I stay at home, I watch TV and my legs and back hurt. Gardening here reminds me of gardening in Laos. I'm Hmong and that's why I still garden. I can't eat hamburgers. I eat homegrown foods."

The Garden Project works with a lot of refugee communities. There are Hmong gardeners, who pass down seeds brought from Asia, African gardeners, who forgo the mango trees of a warmer climate and Bhutanese gardeners with their orange and yellow marigold display. For both refugee and local gardeners, working in a community space is an opportunity to learn about communicating with other cultures. Gardeners have to decide how to share space, if they want to use organic practices and what constitutes "too weedy."[108]

Chickens have not only practical roles as a source of food in the lives of the Hmong but also roles in religious rituals and traditions. Chickens are a favorite food among Hmong people, who also used them for "ritual and healing ceremonies or for weddings. . . . The ability to raise their own chickens for food and ritual purposes gave those involved a sense of control over their lives and made them less dependent on others. Raising chickens, like gardening and foraging, linked 'Old world' activities to the new country and reduced Hmong fears about losing their culture and about being unable to practice their religious beliefs."[109]

At traditional weddings, chickens play an important role. Lian and Kao Xiong showed their wedding photograph from the refugee camp in Thailand. Christine's mother explained the importance of the two chickens. They "finalize the marriage joining the bride and groom."

> A Hmong wedding ritual involves tying a length of white ribbon or string from around the wrist of the bride to around the wrist of the groom. A respected elder or pair of elders performs the tying ritual and accompany themselves with chants. A young hen, rooster, and a hard-boiled egg are also a part of the ceremony as symbols for the coming together of all parts. Candles and burning incense alert the spirit world to the fact that a marriage is taking place. After the hard-boiled egg has been halved, each marriage partner eats one of the halves.

Fishing is a popular sport among the Hmong American males—elderly and younger men and boys. It is a way to "practice subsistence activities in the United States in order to save money." They also hunt squirrel, deer, and game birds to supplement their groceries.[110] However, Hmong Americans also just enjoy fishing and hunting for the sake of the actual sport as well. Websites share information with others about tournaments, fishing and hunting gear, opportunities for outings, and other interesting articles. Fishing and hunting provide one more avenue for Hmong people to connect with one another.

Education Is Key

Education is necessarily interrelated with work for Hmong refugees as they adapt to their new life in Michigan. They know that an education is the key

Kao (left) and Lian (right) Xiong on their wedding day in Thailand. Photo courtesy of Lian and Kao Xiong.

for them to get a job and become self-sufficient as well as for their children. As refugees, the Hmong know they need to learn new skills to find jobs. Farming the land was not sufficient for the middle-aged generation. They attended adult education classes in job-training skills. They participated in classes in English as a second language (ESL). Some pursued college and

graduate education. They all knew that education for their children was critical to their success and that of their families (see appendix 2).

> When they arrived in the United States, the first generation seemed to con-
> sider the American welfare system a kind of military pension for helping
> in the war. . . . It was clear to many that welfare dependency was not the
> way to get ahead in America. While supporting their families on minimal
> monthly welfare payments, Hmong fathers and mothers tried their best to
> acquire language and the job skills necessary to become self-sufficient, but
> the obstacles were formidable.
>
> Yet, every year more Hmong Americans become professionals and
> earn advanced degrees.[111]

People of Hmong origin believed in the "American Dream" and have become politicians, assembly workers, welders, and health care professionals.
"The most important milestone in Hmong integration will be reached when
their stories have been woven into the living memories of this nation."[112]
More and more Hmong are studying for undergraduate and graduate degrees and are going into a variety of fields including information technology, journalism, engineering, teaching, the military, and medicine.[113] "With
freedom and opportunities come incentives to compete and do well. This is
one of the outstanding Hmong traits in life: desire to compete (*sib twv*), to
excel and improve one's living conditions (*sib twv ua neej*)."[114]

Traditionally, the eldest son and his wife and children live with his parents. Furthermore, young adult family members often remain with their
parents or eventually return to their parents' home. For example, although
not the eldest son, Fu Hang, with his wife and children, recently moved back
from Minnesota to live with his parents in Fenton. Such was also the case
with Christine Xiong and her other siblings, who live in the same home with
their parents in St. Johns. In this way, the Hmong not only foster and encourage family unity and strength but also pool their economic resources to help
each other. One large house with many rooms can be far more economical
than each family living in an individual home.

Tru Hang said that he and his wife always stressed education for their
children. They are very proud of their children's academic accomplishments.
Not only did all of them graduate from high school, they all pursued higher

education degrees. The third oldest, Yee Chang Hang, was the first Laotian Hmong to graduate from the United States Military Academy at West Point in 1991 and still serves on active duty with the US Army. He became a Colonel in the US Army on March 3, 2014.

When Tru Hang and his wife came to Michigan, they started with nothing but eventually sent all eight of their children through school. Hang said, "You can make what you want of your life in America through hard work and education."[115]

Tru Hang said that initially none of his children or wife spoke English. "I speak a little. I understand more than I speak. One day, a lady knocked at my door and wanted me to buy the *World Book*. She said that it will help my children. I didn't have $500, but I said I can pay $50 a month. Those books helped my children a lot when they got into the sixth and seventh grades at school. I kept meeting their teachers. My children were doing well."

An exhibit on Michigan residents of Hmong descent opened at the Frankenmuth Historical Museum in May 2010. Both Tru Hang and his son, Fu, spoke at the opening ceremony. Fu said, "My father risked everything for us to have a better life. . . . That is why I decided to stay here in Michigan. This is home to my father now. This is where our roots are now. You have to remember who you are and where you came from."[116]

Each person I interviewed talked about the importance of getting an education or working hard so that their children could get an education. Chue Kue was motivated to leave Thailand to pursue his education and find work in the United States. His thoughts about education and work are inseparable. He took some English classes in Thailand. "While growing up in Laos, I could never have imagined my life changing so dramatically. I could only imagine moving to a neighboring country, but not across the globe. I was clueless what the country will be like, but I thought to myself that I will have the opportunity to go to school."

Chue Kue decided to go into business administration because he believes that every country has to have business, and business is the only way the country will grow. He likes to make his own money instead of working for someone else. He is self-employed doing translation services and is in the insurance business. The question was how would he support his family in this new country? It is a new world, and he did not speak the language. It was a very big problem for him, a great deal of stress and insomnia.

He got a job at the school to help a teacher from the Philippines, but her pronunciation was not the best. He could not understand her most of the time, so he had more stress. He hated the alarm clock in the morning, and started having nightmares about going to school every night. He did not know English himself and could not figure out how he could teach someone else. He wanted to go to day school, but his sponsor wanted him to take night classes and work during the daytime. When he attended school, it was very hard because he could not understand what the teacher said. When he read the text, he had to look at the dictionary word for word. "Life got little bit easier when I got done with my teaching school. I could communicate with others. The only motivation for me was education with the help of my family."

T. Christopher Thao said that he and his family moved from the East Coast to Minnesota, where he finished his bachelor's degree in political science. He then went to law school there and worked as a lawyer for many years. When God called him to the ministry, he went back to school to Bethel Seminary in St. Paul. Then he went to Luther Seminary also in St. Paul to get his Ph.D. in New Testament studies. He said he was driven by learning. God moved him to do his Ph.D. program. It was not something he desired. Luther Seminary accepted him and offered him a full tuition. He then went to pastor a church in California. In 2008, he came to Michigan to pastor at the Warren Hmong Alliance Church. Thao said, "So it was definitely a plan, God's plan. God had everything covered."

Work

Coming to the United States provided the Hmong with numerous different work opportunities that they did not have in Laos or Thailand.

> The political and economic system of the United States has contributed positively to Hmong ability to take the initiative in achieving entrepreneurial success. . . . This is critical at every life stage. Hmong people are not happy with remaining at the same spot. Traditionally, when moving villages, they wanted to find better pastures and more fertile farming land, so they could make a secure living and accumulate wealthy. In the U.S.

capitalist economy, some Hmong have especially thrived by following this age-old migration but now from one city to another, from one life stage to the next in search of better opportunities.

Living in a capitalist economy with private ownership of the means of production and personal profit as main incentives, Hmong appear to have readily adopted free enterprise based on minimal government intervention and an open market.[117]

According to Vang, Hmong Americans have mostly found work in manufacturing, education services, health care, and social assistance and retail trade wherever they have settled.[118] Thirty-seven percent of employed Hmong work in manufacturing. Many Hmong Americans became home health care workers, social service providers, teachers, nurses, and other health care professionals. They also are operators, fabricators, and laborers. In *Bamboo Among the Oaks: Contemporary Writing by Hmong Americans*, editor Mai Neng Moua points out that more and more Hmong in America are now writing in the first person. Hmong entrepreneurial experiences during the war years suggest that, although many come to the United States lacking a cultural background or experience with Western ways, they do not lack experience with capitalism. Their experiences with cash cropping and trading and small business enterprises during relocation and while in refugee camps may very well have set the tone for their adaptive strategies in the United States."[119]

Kou Yang, department chair in Ethnic and Gender Studies and associate professor of Asian American Studies at California State University, Stanislaus, researched the Hmong American community throughout the United States including Michigan by reading and conducting interviews and group discussions.

According to key informants, the Hmong in Michigan have taken a different approach to earning returns from the American free market system. They own and operate more than 100 restaurants, and make use of the diasporic multicultural heritage by offering in their restaurants American, Chinese and Thai foods.

Conversely, in Washington State . . . the Hmong are involved primarily in the flower business. They have learned to grow and sell flowers, an industrial sector with which they had no familiarity before coming to Washington. Many Hmong residing in . . . North Carolina own and operate egg and poultry farms.[120]

However, "there is also considerable diversity within every Hmong American community." For example in Fresno, California, the Hmong Americans are involved in a variety of fields including "university teaching, medicine, dentistry, engineering, anthropology, business enterprises, fast food services and farming.

Although each local Hmong American community may have developed some of its own characteristics, all of them also hold many things in common. They all share the continuity of attempting to preserve the perceived best features of the Hmong language and culture, while they are also in the ongoing process of developing a new Hmong American culture. They have in many ways become Hmong Americans, preserving intrinsic elements of their cultures while adopting many America cultural mores and customs.[121]

Restaurateurs

Perhaps the Hmong Americans in Michigan realized their entrepreneurial initiative and hard work ethic by starting and managing restaurants in Michigan as a logical variation of their interest and comfort level with their connection with food after harvesting their crops. While the elderly maintained their connection to gardening and the land, more middle-aged Hmong people have become entrepreneurial through their involvement in the restaurant business. Furthermore, individuals from one city have collaborated with relatives in other smaller communities to begin new restaurants. In this way, they maintain their connections by working together.

Mark Pfeifer, Hmong Studies Internet Resource Center editor, said that Michigan's Hmong American community has a particular reputation for its entrepreneurial spirit and that they are engaged in the restaurant business more frequently than Hmong Americans living in other states.

Chue Kue said that the Hmong who go into the restaurant business usually do not have a formal education. Cooking is what they know best. Second, most Hmong people do not want to work for someone else. They do not want others to boss them. That is why they start their own businesses.

"In Detroit for example, many Chinese restaurants and takeout businesses are operated by Hmong Americans. Similar developments can be seen in the Twin Cities of Minnesota, including grocery stores and specialty shops. Two Hmong flea markets have opened in St. Paul and attract thousands of shoppers per week, including out-of-state and overseas visitors."[122] The Hmong own and operate over one hundred restaurants in Michigan and have American, Chinese, and Thai foods on their menus.[123]

Fu Hang talked about the Hmong people's entrepreneurial spirit. He said that some government programs and some church organizations helped them thirty years ago in Michigan. However, the great majority of Hmong in Michigan have done it themselves.

"So, basically, everything we have done, we have earned. We have our niche in the restaurant business because the Hmong want to be their own boss. We have to acknowledge the fact that the Hmong community has never asked for a helping hand. Our parents stressed education."

Fu talked about his father's entrepreneurial, hardworking endeavors because of his difficult experiences at a very young age back in Laos. When his father, Tru Hang, was laid off from GM, he needed to figure out what work he would do. He said his father started the whole Hmong restaurant industry with two other clans. Fu's father, his mother's brother, and his cousin went north to Petoskey and started the first Hmong-owned restaurant in the United States in 1981—Chee Peng. Prior to their move to Petoskey, no Hmong Americans lived there. Some Hmong families had been sponsored in Petoskey but had moved away before the restaurant opened. Now over 200 restaurants can be connected to it, including the Szechuan House in Frankenmuth and No Thai with three locations in Ann Arbor and a new one in East Lansing.[124]

Fu explained that these restaurants then branched out in northern Michigan and down to the Tri-Cities—Saginaw, Bay City, and Midland—then Detroit, which was a big hub for Thai food. That is why, he said, the Hmong own so many restaurants and some of the best Thai restaurants: "Mai's Authentic Thai Cuisine at Twelve Miles and Mound in Detroit serves Thai and Vietnamese noodles. Mai's business is hopping, and it's been open for less than a year. Hmong food has its own unique flavor. We live off the land—lots of veggies and pork in our diet. Everyone knows the Chinese food, so that's why my dad started a Chinese restaurant. Thai food is well-known, too."

Typically, Hmong-owned and Hmong-managed restaurants in Michigan feature Chinese or Thai cuisine. However, some of the restaurants in Minneapolis, which has a much greater Hmong American population than does Michigan, do serve authentic Hmong food. The Hmong are determined to make something of the environment in which they find themselves. As Fu says, "Some of my mentors say I wasn't the smartest at things, but I was smartest to take something and make it my own. I have a health care business. Basically, that's the mentality of the Hmong. Chinese food is good. Thai food is good. That's what the Hmong people are good at. Take something good and make it your own."

Hmong American Lisa Her opened the Erb Thai restaurant in Grand Rapids in 2010. From the time she was a child, she learned about Thai cooking from her family, who came from Laos. Then she worked in her family's restaurant in Sterling Heights. She also prepared gluten-free, vegetarian, and vegan foods for those who have special diets.[125]

Owning and managing a restaurant is very hard work. Ying and Chou Xiong owned the Thai Kitchen restaurant in East Lansing for many years until they sold it in 2012. They worked many long hours each day. They worked hard to create a better life for their four children.

While Chou feels the loss of not having an education. She said, "I worked and worked. I had my kids and there was no time for school. So, I missed that. That's why I encouraged my children to go to school and get an education. Otherwise, you have to work too hard. If you have an education, you have a chance to get a better job from nine to five and you have all the time for your kids on the weekend."

Traditions

The New Year celebration is an important time each year for Hmong people to celebrate and preserve their culture and religion, maintain continuity with their family at regional and national levels, and celebrate the harvest of fruits and vegetables in the fall. Its meaning and concept encapsulates many dimensions of the Hmong culture—both the traditional and the contemporary.

While the New Year is an opportunity for socializing, fun, courtship games,

This little girl epitomizes the essence of the Michigan New Year and Cultural Festival 2012 in Pontiac. She is dressed in a traditional Hmong dress and hat and plays a game on her cell phone. Photo by the author.

more importantly, it is a time for the Hmong to honor their ancestors and "domestic spirits of a family. . . . For a shaman, this is the time when he (or she) ritually dispatches his auxiliary spirits (the *neeb*) to the Otherworld for a few days' rest and then welcomes them back again, and there are major rituals associated with this that take place inside a Hmong house at this time."[126]

Traditionally, the Hmong people believe in shamanism. The shaman, a healing practitioner, acts as an intermediary between the spirit and material world.

Shamans are traditional religious experts who have an ability to diagnose illness and cure suffering or other misfortunes such as droughts or famine. The shaman is believed to have the ability to enter into the otherworld by trance or possession and communicate with the spirits there.[127]

The introduction of Christianity often challenges this very identity, the traditional leadership structure and often the traditional authority of men in the family . . . so the issue of the adoption of Christianity becomes conflated with other changes in relation between gender and generations that are taking place in the new lives of the Hmong today.[128]

In 2010, Chou Xiong's younger sister, Maykao Lytongpao, was the president of the Great Lakes Hmong Association and organized the Thirty-Fifth Michigan New Year and Cultural Festival at the Ingham County Fairgrounds in Mason. She was one of my first connections to the Hmong community in Michigan. She graciously invited me to the New Year festival and later met me for coffee. She shared some of the history of the Hmong people as well as her own story.

Maykao Lytongpao said that her grandfather Lue Lee had been the first Hmong mayor in a province in Laos and was also the first Hmong settler in Michigan in 1975 or 1976. Her father had been a colonel in the US Army in Laos. Her cousin Teng Vang was also one of the first settlers in the Lansing area. He and his his extended family were the refugees whom Chris and Mary Dancisak and Betty Marsh helped settle in Lansing when they first arrived. "After the Communists took over Laos, my family and I moved to Thailand when I was nine years old." After living in refugee camps for two years, her family moved to Limoges, outside of Paris, France, where she went to school. Then the St. Matthew Lutheran Church in Bridgeport, Michigan, sponsored her family. She already had extended family in Michigan and the sponsoring organizations worked hard to try to keep families together. She went to college in Saginaw and now teaches in the Detroit Public Schools.

Fu Hang, president of the Great Lakes Hmong Association, and Hue Yang, president of the Hmong Association, cochaired the Thirty-Sixth Michigan New Year and Cultural Festival, 2012–13 at the Ultimate Soccer Arena in Pontiac. They said that the purpose of celebrating the New Year is to preserve the Hmong culture among Hmong Americans, so that the Hmong people do not "forget where they came from and the struggles they faced and overcame.

Two college students dressed in traditional Hmong clothes at the Hmong New Year celebration at the Ingham County Fairgrounds, November 2010. Photo by the author.

Our community has achieved many accomplishments socially and economically, but we still are faced with many challenges and barriers, such as the increase in health issues in our community. We hope that by creating awareness and education, we can better preserve our health."

Interestingly, while the New Year celebration has origins in honoring the ancestors and seeking help from spirits for good health, it also features a contemporary health fair. Fu Hang's wife, May Hang, a nurse practitioner and *manager with CVS Caremark Minute Clinic,* has organized it. People can get their blood pressure checked. About 3,000 people attend the two-day event. Some dress in traditional Hmong outfits, while many wear contemporary, secular clothing.

Many people volunteer at the two-day celebration and participate in fund-raising and organizing the event, which includes an amazing combination of cultural, sports, and social activities. Preteen and high school students participate in fashion, dance, and singing competitions and cultural activities. People in the audience of all ages then go up to the performers and give roses to their favorites. At the festival of 2012–13, musicians perform on flute, mandolin, and guitar.

Beauty pageants are a special feature of the Hmong festivals. They are based not only on physical beauty but talent and answers given during the judge's interviews and to their questions. Hmong beauty pageants actually originated in Long Cheng, Laos, in 1968. Village leaders selected a woman from each village to compete. They wore traditional clothing. First- and second-place winners received crowns. Runners-up received prize money. The pageants took place right before the New Year celebration, so the winner could go with the male military officials to various events. Some of the winners did charity work, including helping wounded soldiers by giving them food and gifts in hospitals and clinics. The pageants then flourished in Laos and continued in the United States.[129]

Sports activities include volleyball, soccer, and flag football. Hmong played the first two games in refugee camps. Adolescents also played a traditional ball-tossing game called *pov pob*—a courting game. Boys and girls talk with each other while tossing the ball back and forth. Younger children also play the game.

Cultural festivals also feature booths where Hmong sell clothes, videos and DVDs, herbal medicines, and a variety of traditional food. These events provide economic opportunities for others as well.[130] Michigan residents of Hmong descent also organize other sports festivals during the year to help build their communities. Some events are for people within the state. Sometimes, the Hmong travel across borders to participate in or watch the tournaments. Soccer and basketball tournaments are popular.[131]

Some of the Hmong Americans have continued the tradition of embroidery once they came to Michigan. For example, the late Ia Moua Yang from Warren was a refugee from Laos and Thailand who eventually came to Michigan via Rhode Island. As a young girl, Ia Moua learned how to sew the *pa ndau* (meaning "flower cloth"), which incorporates a variety of patterns, motifs, and needlework techniques, including appliqué, reverse appliqué, and embroidery. Mastery of the techniques and repertoire of designs and motifs usually takes years, and expert craftsmanship is valued within the community.

She taught *pa ndau* to her daughters, daughter-in-law, and grandchildren, and she has taught others in her community and given workshops

This is one of Ia Moua Yang's textiles in Hmong style called a mola. It has a black background, green leaves, and images including a tree with flowers and several animals, birds, an elephant, and a cow. Photo courtesy of Michigan State University Museum.

to non-Hmong both within Michigan and in other states. She also wrote a handbook with technical and cultural information on *pa ndau*. Ia Moua Yang received a Michigan Heritage Award at the Michigan State University Folk Festival in 2005.

Michigan Heritage Award nominator Carolyn Shapiro stated, "For Ia, weaving and sewing is not just making cloth, it is creating a social fabric. The care of her craft is the care and nurturing of her people. It is the thread that links them to their ancestors and to each other."[132] Some of Ia Moua Yang's tapestries are in the collection of *pa ndau* at the Michigan State University Museum.

The Residential College in the Arts and Humanities (RCAH) at Michigan State University recently sponsored an exhibit (2012) and panel discussion, "Stories in Textiles, Weavings of War" as part of the yearlong "Legacies of War Series." The RCAH hosted this exhibit, which included textiles from Asia, Africa, and North and South America. They represent "an eloquent and powerful testimony of the impacts of modern warfare in our world and the relevancy and resilience of folk arts in contemporary life."[133]

Christine Xiong, an MSU alumna, talked about the Hmong and their tapestries and story cloths. She is one of the daughters of Kao and Lian Xiong and is a member of Lansing's Asian Pacific American Forum. She said, "Traditionally, the Hmong people do not show emotions. They do the tapestries, the 'story cloths,' as a way to express their emotions. My parents always told us that they're going to have a better life for their children."

Postwar Connections

Michigan residents of Hmong descent maintain their pride in having fought side by side with other Americans. As part of the Congressional Record of the 107th Congress, First Session, for July 19, 2001, Michigan senators Carl Levin and Debbie Stabenow recognized the Hmong Special Guerrilla Units. Levin announced that the Lao-Hmong American Coalition, Michigan Chapter, would gather

> to pay tribute to thousands of courageous Hmong who selflessly fought alongside of and in support of the United States military during the Vietnam War. The efforts of the Hmong Special Guerrilla Units were unknown to the American public during the conflict in Vietnam, and the 6th Annual Commemoration of the U.S. Lao-Hmong Special Guerrilla Units Veterans Recognition Day is part of the important effort to acknowledge the role played by the Hmong people in this war.

Levin said,

> While the Special Guerrilla Units may have operated in secret, their efforts, courage and sacrifices have been kept secret for far too long. The word Hmong means "free people," and celebrations such as this Commemora-

tion will raise awareness of the loyalty, bravery and independence exhibited by the Hmong people. . . . These Units, like all those who served the cause of freedom, must know that we appreciate the great sacrifices made by the Special Guerrilla Units.[134]

Stabenow said, "This celebration will also educate future generations of Americans about the sacrifices made by this independent and freedom loving people."[135]

In another instance, the *Oakland Press* reported about a group of Michigan Hmong American veterans who planned a trip to the Air Force Museum at Wright Patterson Air Force Base in Dayton, Ohio, on May 22, 2010.

A museum display of special interest to the veterans is the venerable Cessna 01-E "Bird Dog," the aircraft of choice for the Ravens Forward Air Controllers. The Ravens were an all volunteer group of United States Air Force pilots who spotted and marked enemy targets in Laos for air strikes, by Air Force fighter-bombers flying out of Thailand, and Hmong and Lao pilots flying from Laotian bases.

Hmong observers, called "backseaters," often flew with the Ravens to assist in locating North Vietnamese soldiers, equipment and supplies coming down the Ho Chi Minh trail and destined for South Vietnam, or North Vietnamese divisions that were attacking the Hmong and Royal Laotian forces who opposed the North Vietnamese invasion of the country.

Joua B. Cheng, who lives in Pontiac, was one of many veterans honored during a 1997 congressional ceremony. In addition, he was also a recipient of The Defenders of Freedom Citation, awarded on July 22, 1995, and the Commendation and Citation for Vietnam War Service in Laos, awarded on May 14, 1998. He served as a major in the Hmong army and fought every day during the "Secret War" from 1961–1975.

He was severely wounded three times and returned to combat all three times after he was well enough to resume command of his battalion. After the war, he and his wife, Palee, escaped with their children across the Mekong River to the safety of a refugee camp in Thailand. A church in Petoskey sponsored their emigration to Michigan and they settled first in Petoskey in April 1978 before moving to Saginaw in 1981, and then in 2000 to Pontiac.

One of Joua B. and Palee's sons, Cha Cheng, serves as vice president of the Great Lakes Hmong Association (GLHA), a mutual assistance association dedicated to furthering the well-being of Hmong-Americans via social gatherings, holiday celebrations, English language skills development, and field trips such as the planned visit to the National Air Force Museum.[136]

General Vang Pao died on January 6, 2011, in Clovis, California. Thousands of US residents of Hmong descent mourned his loss. His family requested that an exception be made to the requirement that those interred at Arlington National Cemetery have served in the US military, so that he could be buried there. The US military denied the request.[137] However, a memorial service was held in May 2011 at the Laos Memorial within Arlington.[138]

In 2011, thousands of Hmong in Michigan and throughout the United States mourned the death of their hero. *The Oakland Press* reported that Hmong organizations, including the Hmong of Oakland County Association, the Hmong American Community Inc. of Lansing, Hmong Family Association of Lansing, Hmong Community of Metro-Detroit, and the Lao Veterans of America participated in a special service for him at the Knights of Columbus Hall in Clarkston.[139]

The Next Generation: Dreams and Expectations

Hmong parents want the best for their children. They want them to preserve the Hmong culture and traditions and get a good education. Interestingly, older siblings also often encourage and sometimes even help financially supplement younger siblings' education. Lian Xiong said that Michigan did not have many programs to help the Hmong people, so they were not dependent on a system. She hoped that all her children would have an education. She said they always complained, but if you have too much freedom, you forget school. Without English, it's hard to have job.

Students formed a national organization, the Hmong American Student Association (HASA), in 1996. They have a branch at Michigan State University under the guidance of Professor Joe Cousins. Since 2012, Wayne State University, Grand Valley State University, and Eastern Michigan University have had a HASA on campus. The purpose of the organization is to teach the university community about the Hmong culture and dissipate stereotypes

Christine Xiong (right) with her father, Kao Xiong and her mother, Lian Xiong. Photo by the author.

of them. They help build friends and support one another as they make the transition into the university community away from home.[140]

Christine Xiong graduated from Michigan State University in packaging (2011). Currently, she is a Material Handling Engineer, General Motors-Lansing Delta at Ryder. While still a student, she was president of the MSU chapter of HASA. Christine talked about her parents' dreams and hopes for their children.

> My parents saw coming to America as an opportunity to something good for their family—land of opportunity when they came. This is a better life than what we would have had. That's what they gave us. They said, "We're working hard for you guys. We're doing it passionately. This is a better life because you wouldn't be where you are." Everything they cared about was that we go to school. That was their only expectation. They told us, "We halted our education. We worked so you could go to school. You are our legacy." That's why they worked so hard. That's why they are here. They pride themselves in our education.

Goe Sheng Xiong became president of HASA and in 2012–13 was vice president. Goe Sheng graduated from Michigan State University and now works for Blue Care Network of Michigan. She talked enthusiastically about her participation in HASA and said she wanted to give someone else the opportunity to learn how to manage the association. Hmong students encourage incoming students to perpetuate and promote their culture. They hold an event monthly to help Hmong students connect with others from their same culture. All people are welcome to come to the meetings. Goe Sheng looked at other colleges but MSU was her first choice.

> Unlike the first generation, young people see themselves as urban, cosmo-politan, and technologically savvy. Their identities are a complex weaving of traditional practices and contemporary values. . . . At the same time, we see that some of our students, particularly those who are close to their culture, are becoming strikingly conservative about what is Hmong because they are worried that the language is being lost, the customs are not being honored, the rituals are not being practiced, and so on.

Multicultural university students are now also working on international human rights issues and world environmental protection, "shaping an American future that includes their hopes and dreams."[141]

The Hmong people have been on a long, exhausting journey from Laos, to Thailand, to the United States. What is different about their new home is that they are not fighting a war or living in a refugee camp. Given the few options and opportunities the Hmong have had in the past, perhaps the United States and specifically Michigan have provided a quieter home for these people, not only to resettle and adapt but to flourish, get an education, work, and help their children become educated so they can work and prosper while simultaneously preserving their culture, traditions, and family ties.

Goe Sheng Xiong Strives for Good Education

Goe Sheng Xiong was born in Warren, but she and her family moved to Sterling Heights when she was in the second grade. The school system there was a lot different. In Sterling Heights, she had homework every day except on Friday. Things were a lot more competitive and challenging for her. She said, "Where I am today is probably because of the way that school district was. It was a better community, more high achievers and cleaner."

She does not remember many Hmong families in Warren, and at Sterling Heights she was the only Hmong student until the fourth grade; then there were four or five.

I wasn't really conscious of the fact that my family was from somewhere else when I was back in elementary school. Mom and Dad were stricter. They did not really know how to speak English. They were not as involved as my friends from school. They would try to speak just Hmong to us. My Mom was a little more lenient. They would try to teach us the Hmong alphabet, the sound of the vowels. They tried to make us more aware. But when you're a kid, you just want to have fun. You didn't pay that much attention. You don't care.

I wanted to be able to do the things that all my friends did. They were involved in activities, in sports. My parents said, "No. You go to school and come home. If you do sports, you will get hurt. Just do your homework." Growing up, it was always a struggle like that. My friend was a safety guard. I wanted to be a safety guard. My parents said, "No, you don't need to do that."

Goe Sheng Xiong spent more time with her many cousins than with friends at school, as all their parents visited each other a lot.

Growing up I always knew I wanted to go to college. I think my big brother was a big part of that—my parents too. They always said, "Study hard in school so you can go to college." I took three years of Japanese in high school. I'm good at math and science. They made us do an accelerated program that went through high school.

I want to be out there. Maybe I can work with international business. I chose accounting. I struggle with it a lot, but I love it. My dad wanted me to go to a community college, but I think if anyone can and wants to, they should go to the university. A lot of Hmong people I know go to community college. They get stuck and they have a hard time transferring. I was able to go to MSU because of my siblings; they are more open-minded. I have a lot of cousins with older siblings who are very narrow-minded. They say, "Stay in the family. Be more like Mom and Dad." My siblings said, "You know what you want. So go for it."

My oldest brother gave me money to study. He helped cosign for me. I pretty much did everything myself. I learned how to take care of loans. Whenever I needed money, my parents would try to help. Basically, college is all on me. I'm going to have to pay back everything. To me education is an investment."

Some Afterthoughts

Hmong Americans in Michigan is merely an initial, very brief introduction to the Hmong Americans in Michigan, a backdrop or launch pad for others to explore the history of these people and to conduct future research so that others may learn more about these strong, brave, innovative people. While I interviewed a dozen or more refugees, more than five thousand Michigan residents of Hmong descent live in the state. Each has a story to tell to complement and supplement their people's history in Laos and Thailand and their journey, adaptation, and contributions to Michigan.

The Hmong people have made major transitions and adjustments throughout their lives. They have adapted to a new climate, geography, ethnic groups, jobs, and education. However, what makes the people of Hmong descent so special is not only that they have jumped major life hurdles to adapt to their new lives, but they have also cultivated amazing attitudes and spirits that are so beautiful—warm and inspirational—and that help them transcend their difficult journeys.

As Christine Xiong's mother Lian told us earlier, "We started from nothing. We're newborns coming to the United States. We work very hard. . . . My goal, after speaking English and reading the newspaper, I was determined to keep my children going to school. If my luck, I hope all my children have the education."

As a people, they now have new skills that they never had, as they have not only a spoken voice but a written language to tell their stories and history. It is important now for them and others to tell their story—their recent and ancient history, their culture, their hard work, their thoughts, their ideas, their patriotism, and their commitment and contributions to life in the United States and specifically here in Michigan. In this way, more people will become familiar with the Hmong and learn about these brave people.

The young Hmong American author Kao Kalia Yang beautifully summarizes the essence of the Hmong character and spirit.

> I tell myself: the sun rises so we can do better at what we tried to do the day before. There is no real picture of perfection in doing productive work. Each project, each assignment, each page, each word we write or speak is always only a portrait of us in time in relation to another or many others. Because the sun rises, we receive one more chance to fight to be more effective in the world. The Hmong have words to offer in writing that will stand the test of time, creatively and productively crossing gender, cultural, and linguistic lines of belonging.
>
> I repeat to myself: we can always be only the best of ourselves. If we try and fail, we still live in the same world that created Martin Luther King, Jr., and Rosa Parks, Ronald Takaki and Youa Lee: we try and we fail among those whose lives validate and confirm the power of trying. When we try, the world becomes the best of what we can be as a people.[142]

Appendix 1

Hmong Populations in Michigan Areas

Niles–Benton Harbor metro area 5
Sturgis micro area 2
Marquette micro area 1
Total. *5,875*

Source: Developed by Mark E. Pfeifer based on the 2010 Census of Hmong Populations in Michigan Areas.

Education and Socioeconomic Attainment in the United States

US Hmong Educational Status (2010 American Community Survey): Educational Attainment (Adults 25 and Older)

- 37.7 percent of Hmong American adults have less than a high school diploma, compared to 14.7 percent of the entire US population
- 62.3 percent of all adult Hmong Americans have earned a high school diploma or higher compared to 85.3 percent of the entire US population
- 14.5 percent of adult Hmong Americans have earned a bachelor's degree or higher compared to 28.0 percent of the entire US population
- The percentage of Hmong with a high school diploma and a bachelor's degree have more than doubled since 1990 showing considerable educational progress
- Hmong men's educational attainment still exceeds that of Hmong women, though the gap has narrowed considerably since 1990. Anecdotal evidence suggests women have eliminated the gap and perhaps even pulled ahead in terms of enrollment and completion of higher education

US Hmong Socioeconomic Status (2010 American Community Survey)

- US Hmong median family income in 2010 was $47,465, compared to $62,112 among the entire US population

- US Hmong per capita income in 2010 was $11,012, compared to $26,942 among the entire US population
- 25.3 percent of US Hmong families lived below the poverty level in 2010, compared to 10.5 percent of all US families
- The percentage of US Hmong families living below the poverty level fell from nearly 70 percent to less than 30 percent between 1989 and 2010
- In terms of job distribution, by far the largest percentage of US Hmong adults were concentrated in manufacturing jobs—28.7 percent in 2010. This compares to the 10.7 percent of the entire US adult population who worked in manufacturing jobs
- The US Hmong homeownership rate in 2010 was 46.4 percent up from 13 percent in 1990

Excerpt from Hmong 101 Presentation, written by Txong Pao Lee and Mark E. Pfeifer, PhD, Hmong Cultural Center, Saint Paul, MN (www.hmongcc.org). Used with permission.

Recipes

The first three recipes are from Kou Yang with her mother Pai Thao Yang and her mother-in-law Maly Sayaovang. Kou Yang is from Michigan and now lives in Wisconsin. The last two recipes are from Christine Xiong.

Sweet Pork / Pork Feet (serves 4–5; total cook and prep time approx. 3 hours)

Ingredients

water

2½ cups sugar (keep 1 cup separate)

4 cloves of garlic (minced and smashed)

1 cup of fresh ginger (minced and smashed)

1 Tbsp. salt

6 eggs (hard-boiled and peeled)

3 stalks lemongrass

2 pounds of pork (pork ribs, pork feet, pork ears—any type of meat that you prefer)

Utensils

Crock-Pot, nonstick pan, nonstick pot

Directions

To prepare the eggs:

1. Heat nonstick pan.
2. Pour in 1 cup of sugar.
3. Let sugar melt while stirring until it reaches a very dark brown color. (The sugar will be used only to color the eggs, so don't be afraid if you feel you are burning the sugar.)
4. Once you have achieved the desired color, turn off the heat.
5. Add 1½ cups of water to the sugar. (Warning: this will create steam; do not put your face near. Simply hold the handle and pour from afar.)
6. Once steam goes away, turn the heat back on to medium.
7. When the sugar has liquefied, put in the eggs.
8. Let them simmer in the liquid until the eggs have reached the desired color, occasionally turning them to get even color.

To prepare the meat:

1. Heat nonstick pot.
2. Add 1½ cups of sugar and melt, stirring until it reaches a dark brown color. (Do not burn the sugar.)
3. Once you achieved the desired color, add lemongrass, ginger, and garlic. Cook and stir for 2 minutes.
4. Stir in pork and let it settle for about 5 to 10 minutes, depending on what type of pork you are using (basically until the outside of the pork meat is no longer red).
5. Add 5 cups of water and salt.
6. Cover pot and bring to a boil, then add the eggs.
7. Simmer until the pork is very tender, stirring occasionally. Once tender, it is ready to eat

NOTES: Taste varies; some people like this dish sugary, while others like it light. So adjust taste as desired.

If you are using a Crock-Pot, after step 6 transfer to the Crock-Pot and let it cook on high until tender, or you can cook it longer at a lower temperature—for example if you wanted to make this dish for dinner and you started that morning.

Chicken Laab (serves 4; prep and cook time 1 hour)

Ingredients

3 or 4 chicken breasts

1 packet of Laab-Namtok seasoning mix (can find at any oriental store/ market)

mint or spearmint, minced (approx. 5–6 leaves)

Thai basil, minced (approx. 5–6 leaves)

cilantro, minced (6–8 sprigs)

Asian cilantro, minced (4–5 sprigs)

green onions (only the leaves, 3–4) (shred with fork or toothpick, then cut into 1 inch pieces)

1 or 2 Thai chilis (red or green), cut into pieces (make sure you are wearing cooking gloves)—varies with how spicy you want it

¼ cup or more lime juice (varies on how sour you want the taste)

Directions

1. Cook the chicken meat until tender and juicy—do not make it dry (you can cook the meat any way you want to).
2. Dice chicken and put in a large bowl.
4. Add ¼ cup lime juice.
3. Add half of seasoning packet and herbs with pepper.
5. Mix and taste.
6. Adjust to taste, maybe adding more lime or more pepper.
7. Ready to eat with side of romaine lettuce or iceberg lettuce and rice.

NOTE: you can do this dish the same way with cooked beef. Raw beef uses different ingredients.

Boiled Pork and Mustard Soup

Ingredients

1 pound of pork ribs (or pork meat of choice)

1 or 2 heads of Chinese mustard greens

salt

Directions

1. Fill a nonstick medium pot halfway with water and bring to a boil.
2. Add pork and cover until the liquid boils again or until meat is cooked.
3. Add mustard greens and salt (to taste).
4. Let it cook until mustard greens are soft (not too soft), or to your taste.
5. Usually serve with side of rice.

Tomato Pepper Dish (typically eaten with a side of rice)

Christine Xiong says that vegetarian dishes in Laos are very plain and simple. Most of the time they are either boiled squash or greens fried in oil with salt.

Ingredients

4 large tomatoes
½ cup of cilantro leaves
3 green onions
salt
MSG
Thai chili pepper

Directions

1. Place the tomatoes in a pot and let simmer until they are completely cooked.
2. Set the pot aside until the tomatoes cool.
3. Pulse the green onion and 1 Thai chili pepper (more if you like it spicy) in a food processor.
4. Add the tomato and cilantro leaves. Pulse a few more times then add salt and MSG to taste.

Coconut Rice Wrapped in Banana Leaves (dessert)

Ingredients

2 cups of sticky rice
1 cup of coconut milk
1 cup of sugar
banana leaves

Directions

1. Steam sticky rice until rice is almost cooked. Texture should be dry to the touch and semi-hard. Set aside.

2. In another pot, heat the coconut milk to a simmer.

3. Pour in the sugar and stir until sugar has dissolved. Set pot aside until it is warm to the touch. Pour the coconut milk and sugar over the rice and mix thoroughly.

4. While the rice is cooking, rinse the banana leaves, remove the rough edges, and cut into 6″ × 6″ squares. If the leaves are dry, blanch them in hot water and use quickly.

5. Cut pieces of string about 1″ long.

6. Place a spoonful of the rice mixture on a banana leaf square. Wrap the banana leaf around the rice (similar to how you would wrap an egg roll). Fold in the edges and completely tie the roll with a piece of string so the edges are secure and no rice comes out of the leaf.

7. Place the rolls into a steamer for 15–20 minutes.

NOTE: These are best eaten warm but are also good cold.

Resources

Organizations and Institutions in Michigan

- *Great Lakes Hmong Association.* www.glhainc.org; P.O. Box 210781 , Auburn Hills, MI 48321; (248) 736-8695; email: maykao@GLHAinc.org
- *Hmong Community of Metro-Detroit.* http://www.hmongdetroit.org; P.O. Box 290, Eastpointe, MI 48021
- *Hmong American Community Inc.* 913 W. Holmes Road, Lansing, MI 48910-0426
- *Michigan State University Museum.* You can go to the website to schedule a visit to see Hmong tapestries and jewelry. http://museum.msu.edu/s-program/mtap/Collections/visits.html
- *Hmong American Student Association at Michigan State University.* www.msu.edu/~hasa
- *Hmong Michigan Golfers Association.* 11256 Keith, Sterling Heights, MI 48312
- *Warren Hmong Alliance Church.* 30301 Gloede Dr., Warren, MI; (586) 772-2211

Other Organizations and Institutions

- *HmongHealth.org.* http://www.hmonghealth.org

- *Hmong Cultural Center.* http://www.hmongcc.org
- *Hmong Archives.* www.hmongarchives.org
- *Hmong Studies Journal.* www.hmongstudiesjournal.org
- *Hmong Resource Center Library.* www.hmonglibrary.org
- *Hmong National Development.* www.hndinc.org
- *Lao Family Community of Minnesota.* www.laofamily.org
- *HmongEmbroidery.org.* www.hmongembroidery.org
- *Hmong Kayak Fishing Club.* www.hmongkayakfishingclub.com

Films

- *Gran Torino.* Dir. Clint Eastwood. Warner Bros., 2008.
- *Miao Year.* Dir. William R. Geddes. McGraw-Hill Contemporary Films, 1964.
- *The Place Where We Were Born.* Written by Kao Kalia-Yang.

Exhibits and Collections

- *Hmong Exhibit Text and photos from Frankenmuth Historical Association.* Jonathan Webb (CD).
- *Southeast Asian Hill Tribe Textiles and Hmong American Textiles Collection.* http://museum.cl.msu.edu/s-program/mtap/Collections/hmong.html.

Notes

1. Paul Hillmer, *A People's History of the Hmong* (Minneapolis: Minnesota Historical Society, 2010), 15.

2. Ibid., 8.

3. Chia Youyee Vang, *Hmong America: Reconstructing Community in Diaspora* (Urbana: University of Illinois Press, 2010). "The history of the Hmong people who came to the United States as refugees beginning in the mid-1970s is a history of larger, modern-era political and economic struggles. It is a story of the rise and fall of Chinese dynasties and their interactions with ethnic minorities, of European colonialism and its disintegration during the twentieth century, of nation-building in the former Indochinese colonies, and of American empire-building during the Cold War. Hmong experiences have varied within their own ethnic group and vis-à-vis the larger societies in which they find themselves; however, one constant across place and time is that the Hmong, as a world ethnic minority, have struggled to maintain their ethnic identity. Although they have never had a nation as we know nation-states today, Hmong nation building efforts have been an integral part of their modern history" (150).

4. Lillian Faderman with Ghia Xiong, *I Begin My Life All Over: The Hmong and the American Immigrant Experience* (Boston: Beacon Press, 1998), 10.

5. Jennifer Yau, "The Foreign-Born Hmong in the United States," Migration Policy Institute, Migration Information Source, January 2005 (online).   **83**

6. Kou Yang, "Forging New Paths, Confronting New Challenges," in *Hmong and American: From Refugees to Citizens*, ed. Vincent K. Her and Mary Louise Buley-Meissner (Minneapolis: Minnesota Historical Society Press, 2012), 161.

7. Hmong American Partnership, "Hmong Populations of U.S. Metro and Micro Areas, 2010."

8. Jane Hamilton-Merritt, *Tragic Mountains: The Hmong, the Americans and the Secret Wars for Laos, 1942–1992* (Bloomington: Indiana University Press, 1993). "The Chinese forbade Hmong upon penalty of death to use their written language. Women cleverly kept their alphabet alive including its letters in intricate hieroglyphic-like patterns passed on generation after generation from mother to daughter to adorn tribal dresses. During the years of fleeing and disruption, however, the Hmong lost the ability to use their written language" (5–6).

9. Gary Y. Lee and Nicholas Tapp, *Culture and Customs of the Hmong* (Santa Barbara, CA: Greenwood, 2010). "Throughout the course of this history, the Hmong as a people have struggled fiercely to maintain their own language and identity. . . . The fact that the Hmong lived in the most remote mountain fastnesses . . . itself speaks of a long historical process in which stronger state-based people became dominant at the expense of peoples without writing" (7–8).

10. Tim Pfaff, *Hmong in America: Journey from a Secret War* (Eau Clair, WI: Chippewa Valley Museum Press, 1995). "In the 19th century, the Hmong were not known to have a written language. However, folk stories relate that they once used a written script which was banned by a Chinese emperor. Hmong women were said to have incorporated the characters into their needlework in an attempt to preserve the script" (20).

11. Kurt C. Dewhurst and Marsha MacDowell, *Michigan Hmong Arts: Textiles in Transition* (East Lansing: Folk Arts Division, Michigan State University, 1983). "The written language indeed became hidden as it was not until the late 1950s that missionary workers in Laos began to write down in the Western alphabet the sounds which the Hmong had until that time written only in pictorial form. Although the 'original alphabet' has been lost, the designs remained and have been handed down from generation to generation" (15).

12. Hillmer, *People's History*, 6.

13. According to Her and Buley-Meissner, *Hmong and American*. "An example is unmistakable in the groundbreaking book *Bamboo Among the Oaks: Contemporary Writing by Hmong Americans*, the first anthology of prose and poetry by Hmong Americans to be published for a national audience" (14–15). Mai Neng

Moua, ed., *Bamboo Among the Oaks: Contemporary Writing by Hmong Americans* (Minneapolis: Minnesota Historical Society Press, 2002), 7. In 2011, the Hmong American Writers' Circle (HAWC) edited an anthology *How Do I Begin: A Hmong American Literary Anthology* (Berkeley, CA: Heyday, 2011). Founded in 2004, the HAWC "has served as a forum to discover and foster creative writing within the Hmong community. HAWC coordinates writing workshops and provides educational/professional support and networking opportunities to emerging writers in California's Central Valley. Many of the contributing authors have published their work in major publishing houses throughout the United States" (xii).

14. Kao Kalia Yang, "To See a Bigger World: The Home and Heart of a Hmong American Writer," in Her and Buley-Meissner, *Hmong and American*, 229.

15. Faderman with Xiong, *I Begin My Life All Over*, 1–2.

16. Pfaff, *Hmong in America*, 12.

17. Donald A. Ranard, ed., *Hmong: An Introduction to Their History and Culture* (Washington, DC: Center for Applied Linguistics), chap. 3 (online book).

18. Kou Yang, "Hmong Diaspora of the Post-war Period," *Asian and Pacific Migration Journal* 12, no. 3 (2003): 296.

19. Yang, "Forging New Paths," 170.

20. Faderman with Xiong, *I Begin My Life All Over*, 1–2.

21. Vang, *Hmong America*, 20.

22. Pfaff, *Hmong in America*. "In the 1850s, France looked with envy at British control of the lucrative 'China trade. . . .' By navigating the Mekong and Red rivers, they hoped to bypass the China coast and forge their own alliances in the interior. . . . In the following decades, the French used military might and diplomatic subterfuge to conquer local opposition. By 1893, they had overcome armed resistance in Vietnam, Laos, and Cambodia and established French Indochina" (24–25).

23. Faderman with Xiong, *I Begin My Life All Over,* 4–5.

24. Pfaff, *Hmong in America*, 29.

25. Vang, *Hmong America*, 24.

26. Faderman with Xiong, *I Begin My Life All Over*, 5.

27. Vang, *Hmong America*, 24.

28. Ibid., 24–27.

29. Ibid., 29.

30. Faderman with Xiong, *I Begin My Life All Over*, 7.

31. Vang, *Hmong America*, 30–33.

32. Ibid., 34–35.

33. Ibid., 35.

34. Ibid., 37–38.

35. Sheng-Mei Ma, *East West Montage: Reflections on Asian Bodies in Diaspora* (Honolulu: University of Hawaii Press, 2007), 222–23. Ma quotes from Christopher Hays and Richard Kalish, "Death-Related Experiences and Funerary Practices of the Hmong Refugees in the United States," *Journal of Death and Dying* 18, no. 1 (1987–88): 64–65, referring to "the psychological aftershocks of survival" (222).

36. Kao Kalia Yang, *The Latehomecomer: A Hmong Family Memoir* (Minneapolis, MN: Coffee House Press, 2008), 3–8.

37. Lee and Tapp, *Culture and Customs*, 15.

38. Fungchatou T. Lo, *The Promised Land: Socioeconomic Reality of the Hmong People in Urban America (1976–2000)* (Bristol, IN: Wyndham Hall Press, 2001), 73.

39. Nengher N. Vang, "Political Transmigrants: Rethinking Hmong Political Activism in America," *Hmong Studies Journal* 12 (2011): 14.

40. Vang, *Hmong America*, 41.

41. Keith Quincy, "From War to Resettlement," in Her and Buelli-Meissner, *Hmong and American*, 70.

42. Faderman with Xiong, *I Begin My Life All Over*, 10.

43. Pffaf, *Hmong in America*, 55–56.

44. Jo Ann Koltyk, *New Pioneers in the Heartland: Hmong Life in Wisconsin* (Needham Heights, MA: Allyn and Bacon, 1998), 25. Quoting Dwight Conquergood, "Health Theatre in a Hmong Refugee Camp: Performance, Communication, and Culture," *Drama Review* 32 (3): 180.

45. Lo, *The Promised Land*, 75.

46. Ibid., 76–78.

47. Ibid., 22.

48. Lee and Tapp, *Culture and Customs*, 17.

49. Ibid., 16.

50. Lo, *The Promised Land*, 80–81.

51. Mary Louise Buley-Meissner, "Stitching the Fabric of Hmong Lives," in Her and Buley-Meissner, 238.

52. Ibid., 233.

53. Lo, *The Promised Land*, 83.

54. Buley-Meissner, "Stitching the Fabric," 246–49.

55. Marsha MacDowell, *Stories in Thread: Hmong Pictorial Embroidery* (East Lansing: Michigan State University Museum, 1989), 3.

56. Koltyk, *New Pioneers in the Heartland*, 28–29.

57. Vang, *Hmong America*, 42.

58. Koltyk, *New Pioneers in the Heartland*, 25, quoting Carol A. Mortland, "Transforming Refugees in Refugee Camps," *Urban Anthropology* 16, nos. 3–4 (1987): 379.

59. United Nations High Commission for Refugees, "Convention and Protocol Relating to the Status of Refugees," Article 1. A2. All Souls College, Oxford. Oxford Audio Visual Library of International Law (online).

60. Vang, *Hmong America*, 45.

61. Ranard, *Hmong*, 29.

62. US Department of Health and Human Services, Administration for Children and Families, Office of Refugee Resettlement, "Report to Congress" (Washington, DC: US Publications, 2006), 79 (online).

63. Morton Abramowitz and George Rupp, "A Plea to the World over Hmong Sent Back to Laos," *New York Times*, January 7, 2010 (online).

64. Buley-Meissner, "Stitching the Fabric," 235.

65. Dewhurst and MacDowell, *Michigan Hmong Arts*, 2.

66. Ibid.

67. Erin Patrick, "The US Refugee Resettlement Program," Migration Policy Institute, Migration Information Source, June 2004, 6 (online).

68. Lee and Tapp, *Culture and Customs*, 19.

69. Hillmer, *People's History*, 237.

70. Kathleen Newland, "Refugee Resettlement in Transition," Migration Policy Institute, Migration Information Source, 2002, 2 online article.

71. Cathleen Jo Faruque, *Migration of Hmong to the Midwestern United States* (Lanham, MD: University Press of America, 2002), 7–8.

72. Patrick, "US Refugee Resettlement Program."

73. Vang, *Hmong America*, 47.

74. Ibid.

75. Ibid., 46.

76. Ibid., 47.

77. Ibid., 48.

78. Susan McInerney, "*Gran Torino* Features Former Local Resident," *Frankenmuth News*, March 4, 2009.

79. U.S. Department of Health and Human Services, Administration for Children and Families, Office of Refugee Resettlement "Report to Congress," 82

80. Dewhurst and MacDowell, *Michigan Hmong Arts*, 1–2.

81. Faruque, *Migration of Hmong*, 6.

82. Dewhurst and MacDowell, *Michigan Hmong Arts*, 2.

83. Gary Yia Lee, "Spirit of Enterprise, Emergence of Identities," in Her and Buley-Meissner, *Hmong and American*, 94–95.

84. Faruque, *Migration of Hmong*, 7–8.

85. Ma, *East-West Montage*, 219–20.

86. Mei-Ling Hopgood and Jeff Gerritt, "Gangs Prompt Hmong Plea: How Can We Save Children? Parents Fight to Keep Control, and Teens Deal with Insecurities," *Detroit Free Press*, October 26, 1999 (online).

87. In *Hmong and American: From Refugees to Citizens*, Her and Buley-Meissner write: "All too often, stereotypes are a reality that Hmong in the United States confront in the news, in school, at work, and in other settings where they citizenship is overlooked and their image as an unwelcome refugee remnant of the Vietnam War is reinforced. As we reflect on family and community life, we are continually perplexed by the mismatch between how Hmong view themselves and how others perceive them. Like all other immigrant groups, Hmong people have changed, as has their culture. Yet, this fact proves difficult to communicate when preconceived notions of their identity remain prominent" (12).

88. Associated Press, "Hmong Community Ponders Reducing Gang Violence," *Argus Press*, October 18, 1999 (online).

89. Gran Torino Film Locations, *Gran Torino*, 2008 (online).

90. Ibid.

91. "News Maker Ahney Her," interview by Eric Gallippo, *Lansing City Pulse*, January 21, 2009 (online).

92. Mark E. Pfeifer, John Sullivan, Kou Yang, and Wayne Yang, "Hmong Population and Demographic Trends in the 2010 Census and 2010 American Community Survey," *Hmong Studies Journal* 13, no. 2 (2012): 27.

93. Ibid.

94. Ibid.

95. Robert L. Kaiser, "After 25 Years in the U.S., Hmong Still Feel Isolated," *Chicago Tribune*, December 27, 1999 (online).

96. Dennis Archambault, "Young and Asian in Detroit," *Model D. Media*, November 14, 2006 (online).

97. Ibid.

98. Ibid.

99. Faruque, *Migration of Hmong*, 42.

100. Vincent Her, "Searching for Sources of Hmong Identity in Multicultural America," in Her and Buley-Meissner, *Hmong and American*, 36.

101. Jo Ann Koltyk, *New Pioneers in the Heartland: Hmong Life in Wisconsin* (Needham Heights, MA: Allyn and Bacon, 1998), 107–17.

102. Ibid.

103. Jess Anna Speier, *Hmong Farmers: In the Market and On the Move* (St. Paul, MN: Farmers Legal Action Group, n.d.) (online).

104. Garden Project, Greater Area Lansing Food Bank, *Growing Healthy Food, Cultivating Connections*, 2011 annual report.

105. Rhonda B. Sewell, "Garden Sites Help Families Survive," *Lansing State Journal*, July 13, 1987 (online).

106. Interview with Anne Raucher, former Garden Project director, Greater Area Lansing Food Bank, October 3, 2012.

107. Garden Project, *Growing Healthy Food*.

108. "Refugees Put Down Roots in Lansing Community Gardens," *Spartan Online Newsroom*, November 23, 2011 (online).

109. Koltyk, *New Pioneers*, 116–17.

110. Ibid., 114.

111. Quincy, "From War to Resettlement," 75.

112. Her, "Searching for Sources," 40.

113. Yang, "Forging New Paths," 168.

114. Lee, "Spirit of Enterprise," 91–92.

115. McInerney, "*Gran Torino* Features Former Local Resident."

116. Ibid.

117. Lee, "Spirit of Enterprise," 91.

118. Chia Youyee Vang, "Making Ends Meet: Hmong Socioeconomic Trends in the U.S.," *Hmong Studies Journal* 13, no. 2 (2010): 4.

119. Koltyk, "New Pioneers in the Heartland," 103.

120. Kou Yang, "Hmong Americans: A Review of Felt Needs, Problems, and Community," *Hmong Studies Journal* 4 (2003): 9–10.

121. Ibid.

122. Lee, "Spirit of Enterprise," 92.

123. Yang, "Hmong Americans," 9.

124. Nancy Krcek, Allen "Thai This," *Northern Express*, April 6, 2009 (online).

125. Alex Beaton, "Day 329: Erb Thai," *Awesome Mitten*, April 29, 2012 (online).

126. Lee and Tapp, *Culture and Customs of the Hmong*, 179.

127. Ibid., 24.

128. Ibid., 43.

129. Malisamai Vue, "Hmong Beauty Pageant: From the Past to the Present." Article in author's possession.

130. Vang, *Hmong in Minnesota*, 43–46.

131. Ibid.

132. Michigan State University Museum website, http://museum.msu.edu/s-program/mh_awards/awards/2005IY.html.

133. Flyer from MSU exhibit; and Christine Xiong, panel discussion at the Residential College in Arts and Letters, Michigan State University, September 11, 2012.

134. Senator Carl Levin, "In Recognition of the Hmong Special Guerrilla Units," Congressional Record,107th Congress, First Session, July 19, 2001 (online).

135. Ibid.

136. "Area's Hmong-American Vets to Tour Air Force Museum," *Oakland Press,* May, 17, 2010 (online).

137. *CNN,* February 5, 2011 (online).

138. Steve Magagnini, *"Arlington Ceremony Honors Gen. Vang Pao,"* Merced Sun-Star, May 13, 2011.

139. *"Thousands to Honor Hmong War Hero in Clarkston," Oakland Press,* January 26, 2011 (online).

140. Hmong American Student Organization website, https://www.msu.edu/~hasa/HASAabout.html.

141. Her and Buley-Meissner, *Hmong and American*, 18.

142. Yang, "To See a Bigger World," 231.

For Further Reference

Allen, Nancy Krcek. "Thai This." *Northern Express*, April 6, 2009 (online).

Abramowitz, Morton 'A., and George Rupp. "A Plea to the World over Hmong Sent Back to Laos." *New York Times*, January 7, 2010.

"After 25 Years in U.S., Hmong Still Feel Isolated." *Chicago Tribune*, December 27, 1999 (online)

Alisa, Kaarin, ed. *The Hmong*. Detroit, MI: Greenhaven Press, 2007.

Archambault, Dennis. "Young and Asian in Detroit." *Model D. Media*, November 14, 2006 (online).

"Area's Hmong-American Vets to Tour Air Force Museum." *Oakland Press*, May, 17, 2010 (online).

"Arlington Refuses Burial of U.S. Ally from Vietnam War." CNN, February 5, 2011 (online).

American Hmong Partnership Census. Hmong Populations of U.S. Metro and Micro Areas. 2010.

Associated Press. "Hmong Community Ponders Reducing Gang Violence." *Argus Press*. October 18, 1999 (online).

Barr, Linda. *Long Road to Freedom: Journey of the Hmong*. Bloomington, MN: Red Brick Learning, 2004.

Beaton, Alex. "Day 329: Erb Thai." *Awesome Mitten*, April 29, 2012 (online).

Buley-Meissner, Mary Louise. "Stitching the Fabric of Hmong Lives." In *Hmong and*

American: From Refugees to Citizens, ed. Vincent K. Her and Mary Louise Buley-Meissner. Minneapolis: Minnesota Historical Society Press, 2012.

Cayton, Andrew R. L., Richard Sisson, and Chris Zacher, eds. *The American Midwest: An Interpretive Encyclopedia*. Bloomington: Indiana University Press, 2007.

Cha, Ya Po. *An Introduction to Hmong Culture*. Jefferson, NC: McFarland, 2010.

Chou, Kimberly. "Growing Up Hmong in Detroit." *Michigan Daily*, December 7, 2006 (online).

Cooper, Betsy. "9/11 Commission Urges Immigration and Border Reform." Migration Information Source. 2004. http://www.migrationinformation.org/feature/display.cfm?ID=243.

Cooper, Robert George. *Resource Scarcity and the Hmong Response: Patterns of Settlement and Economy in Transition*. Singapore: Singapore University Press, 1985.

Dewhurst, C. Kurt, and Marsha MacDowell. *Michigan Hmong Arts: Textiles in Transition*. East Lansing: Folk Arts Division, Michigan State University, 1983.

Downing, Bruce, and Douglas Olney, eds. *The Hmong in the West: Observations and Reports*. Minneapolis: University of Minnesota Center for Urban and Regional Affairs, 1982.

Donnelly, Nancy D. *Changing Lives of Refugee Hmong Women*. Seattle: University of Washington Press, 1994.

Entenmann, Robert. "The Myth of Sonom, the Hmong King," *Hmong Studies Journal* 6 (2005): 14.

Faderman, Lillian, with Ghia Xiong. *I Begin My Life All Over: The Hmong and the American Immigrant Experience*. Boston: Beacon Press, 1998.

Faruque, Cathleen Jo. *Migration of Hmong to the Midwestern United States*. Lanham, MD: University Press of America, 2002.

Geddes, William. *Migrants of the Mountains*. Oxford: Clarendon Press, 1976.

Goldfarb, Mace. *Fighters, Refugees, Immigrants: A Story of the Hmong*. Minneapolis, MN: Carolrhoda Books, 1982.

Goodkind, J. R. "Promoting Refugee Well-being: A Community-Based Advocacy and Learning Intervention." Ph.D. dissertation, Michigan State University, 2002.

Gran Torino. Grand Torino Film Locations. 2008. http://www.movie-locations.com/movies/g/GranTorino.html.

Hafner-Hoppenworth, Annette. "Hmong Paj Nntaub: A Comparison of Design Motifs, Color, Size, and Ornamental Construction Techniques between 1977–1979 and 1981–1983." Master's thesis, Michigan State University, 1989.

Hamilton-Merritt, Jane. *Tragic Mountains: The Hmong, the Americans, and the Secret*

Wars for Laos, 1942–1992. Bloomington: Indiana University Press, 1993.

Harris, Judi. "Introduction to Refugee Resettlement." St. Vincent Catholic Charities. Lansing, MM. N.d.

Hein, Jeremy. *Ethnic Origins: The Adaptation of Cambodian and Hmong Refugees in Four American Cities*. New York: Russell Sage Foundation, 2006.

Her, Ahney. "Newsmaker Ahney Her." Interview by Eric Gallipo. *Lansing City Pulse*, January 21, 2009 (online).

Her, Vincent K. "Searching for Sources of Hmong Identity in Multicultural America." In *Hmong and American: From Refugees to Citizens*, ed. Vincent K. Her and Mary Louise Buley-Meissner. Minneapolis: Minnesota Historical Society Press, 2012.

Her, Vincent K., and Mary Louise Buley-Meissner, eds. *Hmong and American: From Refuges to Citizens*. Minneapolis: Minnesota Historical Society Press, 2012.

Hillmer, Paul. *A People's History of the Hmong*. Minneapolis: Minnesota Historical Society Press, 2010.

"Historical Museum Hosting Exhibit on Hmong People." *Frankenmuth News*, March 26, 2009.

Hmong American Writers' Circle, ed. *How Do I Begin? A Hmong American Literary Anthology*. Berkeley, CA: Heydey, 2011.

"Hmong Art: Tradition and Change." Sheboygan, WI: John Michael Kohler Arts Center, 1986.

Hones, Donald F. "Educating New Americans: Hmong Immigrant Lives and Learning." Ph.D. dissertation, Michigan State University, 1997.

Hopgood, Mei-Ling, and Jeff Gerritt. "Gangs Prompt Hmong Plea: How Can We Save Children? Parents Fight to Keep Control, and Teens Deal with Insecurities." *Detroit Free Press*, October 26, 1999 (online).

Hoyt, Lauren, and Anne Goudvis, eds. *Facing Both Ways: Reflections on Growing Up in Two Cultures*. Boulder: Self-published, 1998.

Icon Group International. *Hmong: Webster's Timeline History, 1906–2007*. 2010.

Kaarin, Alisa, ed. *The Hmong*. Detroit, MI: Greenhaven Press, 2007.

Kaiser, Robert. "After 25 Years in the U.S., Hmong Still Feel Isolated," *Chicago Tribune*, December 27, 1999 (online).

Keown-Bomar, Julie. *Kinship Networks Among Hmong-American Refugees*. New York: LFB Scholarly Publishing, 2004.

Koltyk, Jo Ann. *New Pioneers in the Heartland, Hmong Life in Wisconsin*. Needham Heights, MA: Allyn and Bacon, 1998.

Kwon, Sylvia E. "Recognition, Identity Construction, and Second-Generation Hmong

American Students in an Urban High School." Ph.D. dissertation, University of
Michigan, 2006.

Lai, Eric, and Dennis Arguelles. *The New Face of Asian Pacific America: Numbers,
Diversity and Change in the 21st Century.* Los Angeles: UCLA Asian American
Studies Center, 2003.

Lee, Gary Yia. "Diaspora and the Predicament of Origins: Interrogating Hmong Post
Colonial History and Identity." *Hmong Studies Journal* 8 (2007): 1–25.

———. "Spirit of Enterprise, Emergence of Identities." In *Hmong and American:
From Refugees to Citizens,* ed. Vincent K. Her and Mary Louise Buley-Meissner.
Minneapolis: Minnesota Historical Society Press, 2012.

Lee, Gary Yia, and Nicholas Tapp. *Culture and Customs of the Hmong.* Santa Barbara,
CA: Greenwood, 2010.

Lee, Txong Pao, and Mark Pfeifer. "Building Bridges: Teaching about the Hmong in
Our Communities." St. Paul, MN: Hmong Cultural Center, 2009-10.

Lindsay, Jeff. "The Hmong in America: A Story of Tragedy and Hope," November 12,
2010. http://www.jefflindsay.com/Hmong_tragedy.html.

Livo, Nomra J., and Dia Cha, comps. *Folk Stories of the Hmong: Peoples of Laos, Thailand, and Vietnam.* Englewood, CO: Libraries Unlimited, 1991.

Lo, Fungchatou T. *The Promised Land: Socioeconomic Reality of the Hmong People in
Urban America (1976–2000).* Bristol, IN: Wyndham Hall Press, 2001.

Ma, Sheng-Mei. *East-West Montage: Reflections on Asian Bodies in Diaspora.* Honolulu: University of Hawaii Press, 2007.

MacDowell, Marsha. *Stories in Thread: Hmong Pictorial Embroidery.* East Lansing:
Michigan State University Museum, 1989.

Magagnini, Steve. "Arlington Ceremony Honors Gen. Vang Pao." *Merced Sun-Star,*
May 13, 2011.

"Mark Pfeifer Returns to St. Paul." *Asian American Press,* November 11, 2011 (online).

Martin, David. *The US Refugee Program in Transition.* Migration Information Source.
2005. http://www.migrationinformation.org/Feature/display.cfm?id=305.

McInerney, Susan. "*Gran Torino* Features Former Local Resident." *Frankenmuth
News,* March 4, 2009.

"Michigan Hmong." *Michigan Daily,* September 20, 2011 (online).

Miyares, Ines M. *The Hmong Refugees Experience in the United States: Crossing the
River.* New York: Routledge, 1998.

Moore, David L. *Dark Sky, Dark Land: Stories of the Hmong Boy Scouts of Troop 100.*
Eden Prairie, MN: Tessera Publications, 1989.

Moore-Howard, Patricia. *The Hmong, Yesterday and Today.* Sacramento, CA: Author, 1982.

Mote, Sue Murphy. *Hmong and American: Stories of Transition to a Strange Land.* Jefferson, NC: McFarland, 2004.

Moua, Mai Neng. *Bamboo Among the Oaks: Contemporary Writing by Hmong Americans.* Minneapolis: Minnesota Historical Society Press, 2002.

Patrick, Erin. "The US Refugee Resettlement Program." Migration Policy Institute, Migration Information Source, June 2004 (online).

Newland, Kathleen. "Refugee Resettlement in Transition." Migration Information Source. 2002. http://www.migrationinformation.org/Feature/print.cfm?ID=52.

Pfaff, Tim. *Hmong in America: Journey from a Secret War.* Eau Clair, WI: Chippewa Valley Museum Press, 1995.

Pfeifer, Mark E. *Hmong-Related Works, 1996–2006: Annotated Bibliography.* Lanham, MD: Scarecrow Press, 2007.

Pfeifer, Mark E., John Sullivan, Kou Yang, and Wayne Yang. "Hmong Population and Demographic Trends in the 2010 Census and 2010 American Community Survey." *Hmong Studies Journal* 13, no. 2 (2012): 1–31.

Quincy, Keith. *Hmong: History of a People.* Spokane: Eastern Washington University Press, 1988.

———. *Harvesting Pa Chay's Wheat: The Hmong and the America's Secret War in Laos.* Spokane: Eastern Washington University Press, 2000.

———. "From War to Resettlement." In *Hmong and American: From Refugees and Citizens*, ed. Vincent K. Her and Mary Louise Buley-Meissner. Minneapolis, Minnesota Historical Society Press, 2012.

Ranard, Donald A., ed. *The Hmong: An Introduction to Their History and Culture.* Washington, DC: Center for Applied Linguistics, 2004.

Ratliff, Martha. "Southeast Asian Languages in Michigan and Ohio." Unpublished paper. Wayne State University, 2001 (online).

———. *Hmong-Mien Language History.* Canberra: Pacific Linguistics, 2010.

Refugee Development Center. "A Glimpse into Our World." 2009. http://www.refugeedevelopmentcenter.com.

"Refugees Put Down Roots in Lansing Community Gardens." *Spartan Online Newsroom*, November 23, 2011.

Religion and Expressive Culture—Hmong." N.d. Everyculture.com.

Schein, Louisa, and Va-Megn Thoj. "*Gran Torino*'s Boys and Men with Guns: Hmong Perspectives." *Hmong Studies Journal* 10, no. 1 (2009): 52.

Scripter, Sami, and Sheng Yang. *Cooking from the Heart: The Hmong Kitchen in America*. Minneapolis: University of Minnesota Press, 2009.

Sewell, Rhonda B. "Garden Sites Help Families Survive." *Lansing State Journal*, July 13, 1987.

Speier, Jess Anna. *Hmong Farmers: In the Market and On the Move*. St. Paul, MN: Farmers Legal Action Group, n.d.

"Thousands to Honor Hmong War Hero in Clarkston." *Oakland Press*, January 26, 2011 (online).

Trueba, Henry T., Lila Jacobs, and Elizabeth Kirton. *Cultural Conflict and Adaptation: The Case of Hmong Children in American Society*. New York: Routledge, 1990.

United Nations High Commission for Refugees. "Convention Related to the Status of Refugees." All Souls College, Oxford. Oxford Audio Visual Library of International Law. 2012 (online).

US Department of Health and Human Services, Administration for Children and Families, Office of Refugee Resettlement. "Report to Congress." 2006. Washington, DC: US Publications.

US Department of Health and Human Services, Office of Refugee Settlement. Refugee Services throughout Michigan. http://www.acf.hhs.gov/programs/orr/data/state_mi_ffy09.htm.

US Office of Refugee Resettlement. *The Hmong Resettlement Study*. Vol. 1: *Final Report*. Minneapolis: University of Minnesota, 1985.

Vang, Chia Youyee. *Hmong in Minnesota*. Minneapolis: Minnesota Historical Society Press, 2008.

———. *Hmong America: Reconstructing Community in Diaspora*. Urbana: University of Illinois Press, 2010.

———. "Making Ends Meet: Hmong Socioeconomic Trends in the U.S." *Hmong Studies Journal* 13 (2012): 1–20..

Vang, Nengher N. "Political Transmigrants: Rethinking Hmong Political Activism in America." *Hmong Studies Journal* 12 (2011): 1–46.

Vang, Thomas. *A History of the Hmong: From Ancient Times to the Modern Diaspora*. Raleigh, NC: Lulu Press, 2008.

Vue, Malisamai. "Hmong Beauty Pageant: From the Past to the Present." N.d. Article in author's possession.

Warner, Roger. *Shooting at the Moon: The Story of America's Clandestine War in Laos*. South Royalton, VT: Steerforth Press, 1996.

Yang, Ia Moua, and Carol Shapiro. *The Pa Ndau of Ia Moua Yang: Keeping Alive the*

Treasure of the Hmong. Self-published, 2002.

Yang, Jerry, with Mark Tabb. *All In*. Colorado Springs: Medallion Press, 2011.

Yang, Kao Kalia. "To See a Bigger World: The Home and Heart of a Hmong American Writer." In *Hmong and American: From Refugees to Citizens*, ed. Vincent K. Her and Mary Louise Buley-Meissner. Minneapolis: Minnesota Historical Society Press, 2012.

———. *The Latehomecomer: A Hmong Family Memoir*. Minneapolis, MN: Coffee House Press, 2008.

Yang, Kou. "Hmong Americans: A Review of Felt Needs, Problems, and Community Development." *Hmong Studies Journal* 4 (2003): 1–23.

———. "Hmong Diaspora of the Post-war Period." *Asian Pacific Migration Journal* 12, no. 3 (2003): 271–300.

———. "Research Notes from the Field: Tracing the Path of the Ancestors—a Visit to the Hmong in China." *Hmong Studies Journal* 6 (2005): 1–38.

———. "Forging New Paths, Confronting New Challenges." In *Hmong and American: From Refugees to Citizens*, ed. Vincent K. Her and Louise Buley-Meissner. Minneapolis: Minnesota Historical Society Press, 2012.

Yau, Jennifer. "The Foreign-Born Hmong in the United States." 2005. Migration Information Source.

Interviews

Dancisak, Chris. August 30, 2012. Lansing, MI. Cochair, sponsorship committee for St. Michaels Church in Grand Ledge, MI; retired director of community relations, Michigan Historical Museum.

Hang, Fu. January 31, 2012. Fenton, MI. Son of Tru and Li Hang; Great Lakes Hmong Association.

Hang, Tru, January 31, 2012. Fenton, MI. Retired military officer with CIA; retired GM employee; founder of numerous restaurants in Michigan.

Harris, Judi. January 13, 2012. Lansing, MI. Director, Refugee Services, St. Vincent Catholic Charities, Lansing.

Hepp, Patricia. November 28, 2011. East Lansing, MI. Retired director, Catholic Social Services, Lansing, MI.

Kue, Yong Chue. October 2, 2011. Madison Heights, MI. President of Hmong Community of Metro-Detroit; insurance salesman.

Lytongpao, Maykao. December 30, 2010. Clarkston, MI. Teacher in Detroit schools;

Great Lakes Hmong Association.

Raucher, Anne. October 3, 2012. Lansing, MI. Former Garden Project director, Greater Area Lansing Food Bank.

Thao, Timothy (Teng C. Thao). October 25, 2011. Warren, MI. Pastor, Warren Hmong Alliance Church.

Tran, Nghia. January 13, 2012. Lansing, MI. Health Coordinator, St. Vincent Catholic Charities, Health Care, Lansing, MI.

Vue, Nanci (Yang). January 13, 2012. Lansing, MI. Nurse and wife of late Tom Vue.

Vue, Tom Cheng. February 19, 2011. Lansing, MI (deceased). Founding member of the Hmong Family Association of Lansing; husband of Nanci Yang Vue.

Vue, Tong. September 25, 2012. Lansing, MI. Christine Xiong's maternal grandmother; Mother of Lian Xiong.

Webb, Jonathan. January 28, 2011. Frankenmuth, MI. Director, Frankenmuth Historical Association.

Xiong, Chou. July 2, 2012. East Lansing, MI. Former owner with her husband, Ying Xiong, of Thai Kitchen, East Lansing.

Xiong, Christine. October 18, 2011. East Lansing, MI. Graduate of Michigan State University in packaging; Material Handling Engineer, General Motors–Lansing Delta at Ryder.

Xiong, Goe Sheng. July 1, 2012. East Lansing, MI. Graduate of Michigan State University, works for Blue Care Network of Michigan.

Xiong, Kao. July 4, 2012. St. Johns, MI. Whitney Auto Air employee, Christine Xiong's father.

Xiong, Lian. July 4, 2012. St. Johns, MI. Whitney Auto Air employee; Christine Xiong's mother; wife of Kao Xiong.

Index